NEEDLEWORK MAGIC

Over 25 Original Embroidery
Projects for Your Home

JANE ILES

Trafalgar Square Publishing
NORTH POMFRET, VERMONT

First published in the United States of America in 1993
by Trafalgar Square Publishing, North Pomfret, Vermont 05053.

First published in Great Britain by Ebury Press

Editor: Valerie Buckingham

Designers: Sue Storey and Patrick McLeavey

Photography: Shona Wood (front jacket and all photographs other than those listed here)

Additional photographs by Jan Baldwin (pages 26–7, 39, 59); and Julie Fisher, styled by Jacky Boase (pages 2 and back jacket, 74–5, 93)

Illustrations: Coral Mula, Elsa Willson

Charts: Debby Robinson

Library of Congress Cataloguing Card Number: 92–64451

ISBN: 0 943955 64 5

Filmset in Linotron Plantin by Textype Typesetters, Cambridge
Printed and bound in Italy by New Interlitho S.p.a., Milan

Contents

To Thomas

Introduction

In writing this book I have tried to do two things. First, to provide you with a variety of original and beautiful projects that range from the simple to the more complex. Each one is intended to beautify your home and to give you hours of pleasure both during its creation and on completion wherever it is displayed.

Secondly, I hope that by seeing my ideas and how I have interpreted them you will develop and nurture an understanding and sensitivity towards the fascinating craft of creative needlework. You will, I am sure, develop a keen eye for those things around you that you find pleasing and that could be used as the inspiration for your own designs and, gradually, I hope you will fill your home and those of your friends with the delights of an embroidery enthusiast.

As with my other books you will see that many of the designs are executed with simple techniques and stitches so that the shapes and colours of each design are emphasised rather than submerged in fancy stitches and indulgent techniques.

In the following pages you will see how I have gathered together a collection of projects that have been inspired by a variety of natural forms. Whether they are flowers and plants or birds and beasts, all have excited me into creating something in fabric and thread. Each project has been inspired not directly from nature but from someone else's ideas; from the patterns around an ancient porcelain dish to printed fabrics and samples of exquisite embroidery. Much of my source material is displayed in the Victoria & Albert Museum, London, a Pandora's box for anyone seeking ideas. But also I found many delightful ideas in pieces of decorated china and porcelain that my grandfather lovingly gathered around him, from country-house sales in East Anglia earlier this century. I have found that a worthless, cracked plate or chipped cup can be as inspiring as a priceless museum exhibit.

Finally, I hope you will enjoy this collection whether you are an enthusiastic novice creating your first Cross-Stitch towel border or an accomplished veteran piecing together the trinket boxes or patchwork sachets. I am sure you will find something that inspires you as it has me.

And remember, feel free and confident to experiment with the designs. Many can be easily adapted by changing fabric and thread, or the scale of design, so that you effectively create your own personal interpretation of my ideas.

Wading Birds Towel Border

Cross Stitch is a simple but effective technique as you can see in this project of few colours and a charmingly naïve repeat pattern. The source of the design was two examples of Chinese 'Export' porcelain which, as the name suggests, is ware that was produced in China and then sent out of the country, in this case to England. I took the inner repeat pattern of the wading birds and stylized water plants from a blue and white border design around a large dish of the Ming period, while the simple heart-shaped patterns on either side have been loosely adapted from the geometric patterns around a vase of the same colouring.

Only four shades of blue have been used in this Cross Stitch design. If you would like to work the design in the alternative Chinese red colourway I have given the substitute thread colours at the end of the project.

MATERIALS

White Hardanger fabric (9 threads per cm, 22 per in), 25 × 66 cm (10 × 26 in). You can use any similar evenweave fabric if it has the same or similar gauge.
White hand towel, 56 cm (22 in) wide
Coats Anchor stranded thread: 2 skeins each Blue 128, 121, 122, 127
White sewing thread
Small rotating frame, or wooden embroidery hoop, 20 cm (8 in) diameter

Stitches used: *Cross Stitch, machine Satin Stitch, Slip Stitch.*

TO MAKE THE TOWEL BORDER

1 If you are using a rotating frame mount the short ends of the Hardanger fabric on the rotating sides of the frame and roll the excess fabric around one of these sides. If you are using a hoop place one end of the strip within the hoop. (You will find that you will have to reposition this several times as you work the border. Similarly, with the rotating frame you will have to adjust the position of the fabric by unrolling and then rolling it around the rotating sides.)

2 Approximately 2.5 cm (1 in) in from the end of the strip of fabric find the centre of the width and mark it temporarily with a dressmaker's pin. This will help you position your Cross Stitch border design centrally along the strip of fabric.

3 Use three strands of thread while you work the border. Remember to work your Cross Stitches so that all the upper stitches face the same way to produce an even effect.

4 Count outwards from the marked centre of your fabric to establish where to start stitching the border heart patterns on either side of the bird design.

Work these hearts by simply repeating the motifs over and over again. Then fill in the central repeat pattern of the wading birds.

If you look carefully at the chart (see page 11) you will see that the bird section of the border design repeats itself every 89 squares or Cross Stitches whereas the outer heart patterns do not repeat themselves within this multiple, so that when you have worked the bird repeat and are about to begin it again the position of the hearts will not coincide with the position shown on the chart. This does not matter, simply continue repeating them along the length of the fabric.

To work the design to fit the width of your hand towel you will have to repeat the bird design nearly three times. When nearing the end of the strip, measure the exact width of your hand towel and work the border to fit.

5 Remove the fabric from the frame or hoop and press it carefully on the

wrong side, using a steam iron.
6 With the Cross-Stitch border centrally positioned, cut away the surplus fabric along both sides to give a strip which is 14 cm (5½ in) wide. Also trim the surplus fabric at the end of the border, leaving 1 cm (⅜ in) at each end for a small turning.
7 Pin and baste the Cross-Stitch border across one end of the towel, tucking in the turned allowance along both short edges. With white sewing thread, machine Satin Stitch along the raw edges of the border, covering them completely with the width of the Satin Stitch and attaching the strip to the towel securely.
8 Finally, Slip Stitch the turned allowance to the towel sides to complete your Wading Bird Hand Towel.

If you wish to make a matching set of bath linen you can easily do so by working a narrow border of the open, lighter, heart pattern for a face cloth. A further variation can be produced by repeating this simple pattern with a mirror image strip of the same pattern to give a double border (see the small guest towel in the photograph). These strips can then be attached in the same way as the hand towel border.

See page 8 for instructions on how to work the chart opposite.

In addition to the blue and white towels I made another striking set of bath linen by using shades of Chinese Red stranded thread on white Hardanger fabric appliqued on to matching towelling. Substitute the shades of blue used on the chart with the following: Coats Anchor stranded thread, Light Red 6, Mid Red 10, Red 13, Dark Red 22.

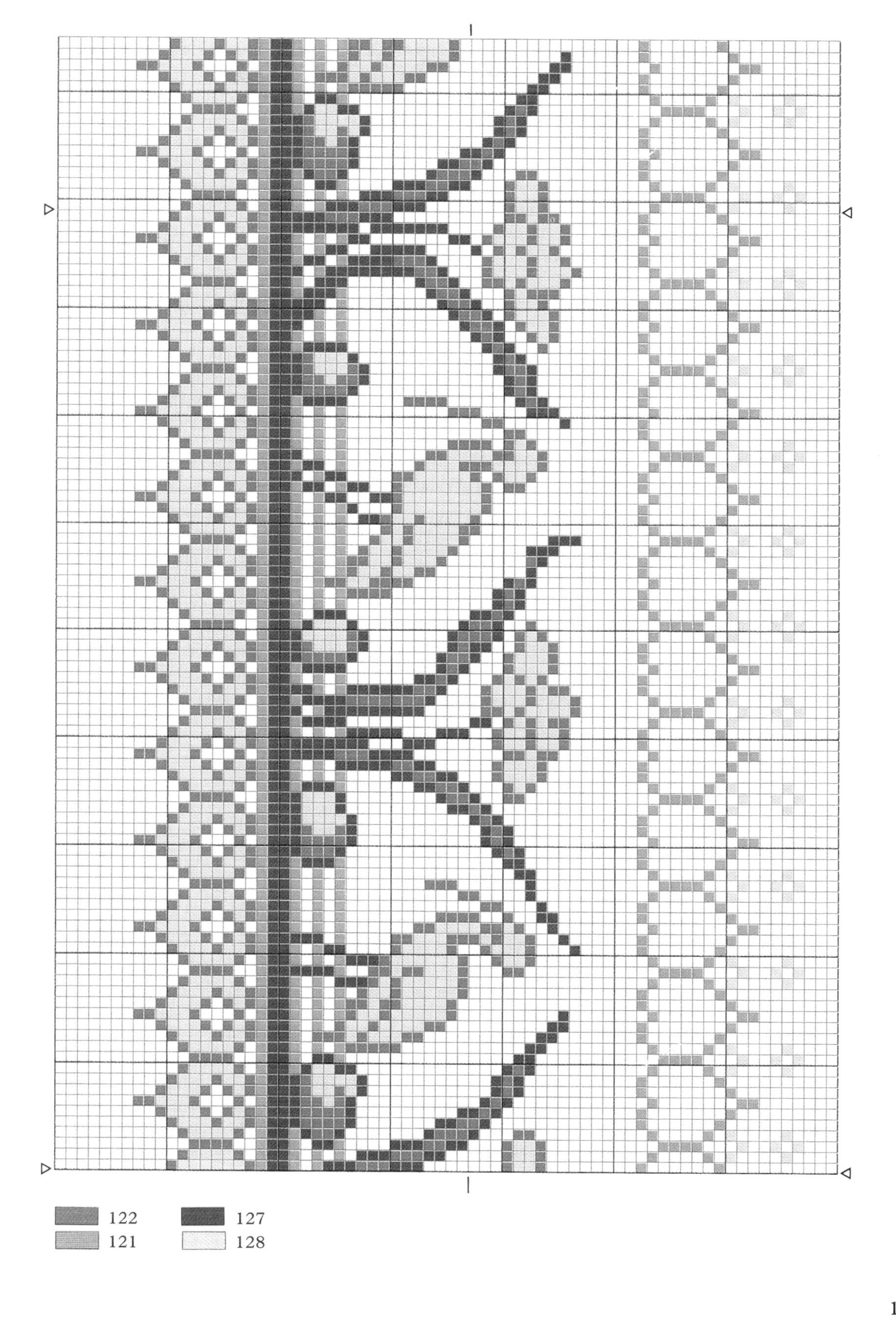
122
127
121
128

Shell and Fish Table Mats

The graceful shapes of shells and fish inspired me to make these lively place mats and matching drinks mats. The source of the design is a large porcelain dish decorated with a wide variety of marine creatures. The painterly qualities of the dish inspired me to use fabric transfer dye crayons to produce a soft and pleasing result. The design, once crayonned and transferred on to fabric, has been quilted with Back Stitches and French Knots and then made up into the mats. I find this method of using transfer crayons (see also page 68) and quilting or outlining a quick and very effective method of stitchery and one that does not require hours and hours of fastidiously close work.

MATERIALS

(to make one mat of each size)

White cotton sheeting, 40 × 100 cm (16 × 39 in)
Terylene wadding, medium weight, 40 cm (16 in) square, and 20 cm (8 in) square
Terracotta red backing fabric, 33 cm (13 in) square, and 15 cm (6 in) square
Heavyweight (pelmet) interfacing, Vilene, 33 cm (13 in) square, and 15 cm (6 in) square
Coats Anchor stranded embroidery thread: 2 skeins each Blue 122, 178; 1 skein each Blue 117, Orange 326, Gold 307
Terracotta red bias binding, 2 m (2¼ yd) long and 12 mm (½ in) wide
Sewing thread to match bias binding
Basting thread
Tracing paper, 33 cm (13 in) square, and 15 cm (6 in) square
Crayola fabric transfer dye crayons
Fine-tipped black felt pen
Embroidery frame, 38 cm (15 in) square or equivalent hoop
Wooden embroidery hoop, 17 cm (7 in) diameter

Stitches used: *Back Stitch, French Knots, Diagonal Basting Stitch, Slip Stitch.*

TO MAKE THE MATS

1 Trace with the felt pen the small drinks mat design on to the centre of the smaller piece of tracing paper. Trace the section of the table mat on to the larger sheet of tracing paper, positioning it so that you can then repeat it twice more overlapping the prawns to produce a complete circular design. To help you position the table mat design on your sheet of paper bear in mind that the completed circle is approximately 30 cm (12 in) in diameter.

2 Measure and cut out the white cotton sheeting to give two squares each measuring 40 cm (16 in) square and then divide the remaining piece in half to give two smaller 20 cm (8 in) squares.

3 Following the crayon manufacturer's instructions (also see Special Techniques, pages 135–6), make a test strip of the different colours which can be achieved with the dye crayons. (Make your small test strip along one edge of one of the larger squares of white fabric.) Remember you need to achieve a variety of blue shades and pale golden-orange shades.

When you feel confident with your results use the crayons to colour in the underside of the two traced designs (refer to the photograph on page 13 to help you to achieve a pleasing effect). Vary the colours of the shells to add interest to your design.

4 Press your white fabric to remove any creases and reserve one large and one small square. Again following the crayon manufacturer's instructions, carefully transfer the two designs on to

the appropriate pieces of fabric. Remember to place the transfer waxy side down on to the fabric and take great care not to move the transfer paper as any movement will create a blurred and unsatisfactory image.

5 Stretch the remaining large square of white fabric on to your embroidery frame. Gently smooth the large square of wadding over this and finally stretch the large transfer design piece over it and fix it in position using staples or thumb tacks. Do not stretch it too tightly as this will squash the wadding and flatten it, reducing the quilted effect that you are going to produce.

6 Prepare the smaller design in the small hoop by sandwiching the wadding between the backing square and the piece of fabric with the small design on it. Baste the layers together using Diagonal Basting Stitches (see Special Techniques, page 137) and then stretch them within the hoop, pulling the layers of the fabric gently to create a smooth effect that is quite taut but still puffy. If you are using a large hoop prepare your layers of fabric and wadding in this way.

7 You are now ready to begin the embroidery. Use two strands of thread throughout the designs and, following the colouring of the trace-off pattern as a rough guide, work around all the

178
122
117
326
307

shapes of each design in small and even Back Stitches. Use French Knots to highlight the eyes of the fish and prawns and also on some of the tiny circular shells. You do not have to follow the colour plan strictly, simply balance the use of the different shades of blue and use the gold and orange threads to outline the shells and star shapes appropriately.

You will find that where you have an intense area of stitching then the quilted effect becomes quite flat but the more open areas, such as the centre of the larger design, delightfully puffy.

8 Once you have completed all the embroidery remove the two pieces of work from the frame and hoop. Do not press the designs, you do not want to flatten them.

9 Using your traced patterns as templates cut out a large circle and a small one from the heavyweight interfacing. Add 6 mm (¼ in) binding allowance all around each circle. Using these interfacing circles as templates, then cut out a backing fabric circle to match each size. Trim away the excess fabric around the two embroidered and quilted designs to match the interfacing shapes.

10 Sandwich the layers together so that the interfacing lies between the backing fabric and the quilted circles (right sides outside). Smooth the layers together and baste to hold around their edges.

11 Fold the bias binding in half around the curved raw edges of one of the mats. Remember to fold in a small turning to neaten the cut end of the binding. Then with matching sewing thread carefully and invisibly Slip Stitch the binding edge to the right side of the mat close to the outermost line of Back Stitches. Trim off the excess binding and neaten the raw ends so that the join is almost invisible, then Slip Stitch the other edge of the binding to the wrong side of the mat stitching through the backing fabric and into the interfacing layer.

Repeat this process with the other mat using the remaining length of bias-binding tape.

Trace-off patterns for the Drinks Mat (left) and Place Mat (right). Trace each design on to tracing paper and remember to use the dye crayons on the reverse side of the traced design. For the larger design, draw and repeat the segment three times, overlapping the prawns and so on to produce a complete circle. Do not trace the dotted guideline showing how the pattern repeats.

Prunus Blossom Box

This charming box, ideal for keeping small pieces of jewellery in, is made totally of fabrics and yarns; no cardboard has been used to stiffen the box, the thickness of the quilted layers and the use of heavyweight interfacing gives it enough rigidity to make it stand up and keep its shape.

I took the design for the embroidery from a small porcelain plate, a piece from my grandfather's collection gathered from country house sales in Norfolk earlier in this century.

I transferred the pattern around the box and on its lid on to the silky fabric with a fabric transfer dye crayon. Then I outlined and highlighted the coloured shapes with Back Stitches and, at the same time, quilted the fabric over a layer of wadding to give a gently raised effect.

Take off the lid and peep inside the box and you will find a surprise drawstring top to the lining.

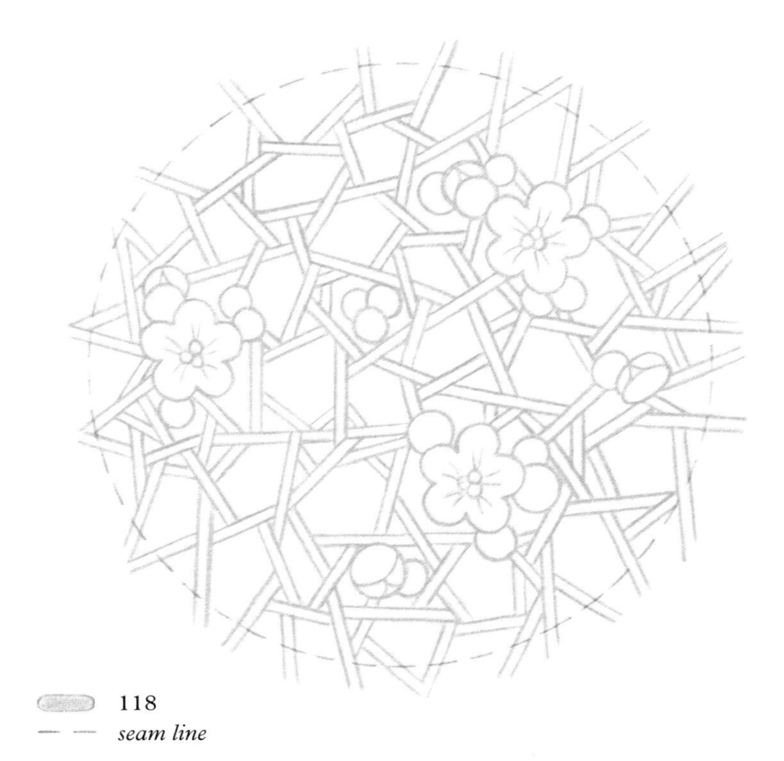

Trace-off pattern for the lid. The dotted line represents the seam line.

MATERIALS

White silky-type synthetic fabric, 25 × 50 cm (10 × 20 in)
White cotton backing fabric, 25 × 50 cm (10 × 20 in)
Medium-weight terylene or polyester wadding, 20 × 46 cm (8 × 18 in)
Royal-blue silky-type lining fabric, 30 × 33 cm (12 × 13 in)
Heavy-weight interfacing, (Vilene), 18 × 22 cm (7¼ × 8½ in)
Coats Anchor stranded embroidery thread: 2 skeins Blue 118
Coats Coton Perlé thread: 1 skein Blue 132
Blue sewing thread to match lining fabric and Coton Perlé basting thread
Good-quality tracing paper
Black fine-tipped felt pen
Blue Crayola fabric transfer dye crayon
Knitting needle
Safety pin
Embroidery frame, 20 × 46 cm (8 × 18 in) rectangular frame or small rotating frame or other suitable frame

Stitches used: *Back Stitch, Fly Stitch, French Knots, machine Straight Stitch, Slip Stitch, Buttonhole Stitch.*

TO MAKE THE QUILTED FABRIC AND BOX

1 Press all the fabrics to remove any creases. Stretch the white cotton backing fabric over the frame ensuring the straight grain lies parallel to the sides of the wooden frame.

2 Lay the wadding over the stretched fabric and smooth the layers together. If you are using a staple gun or tacker hold the wadding gently to the frame around its sides with a few staples but do not pull the wadding completely taut as you want it to remain soft and puffy.

3 Accurately trace the rectangular and circular design shapes on to two pieces of tracing paper, using the fine-tipped felt pen.

4 Use the dye crayon to make a test strip to see the strength of the colour on the particular fabric you are using. Follow the crayon manufacturer's instructions to transfer the marks on to one corner of the white fabric (also see page 135). When you are satisfied that you can achieve the correct strength of colour then very carefully shade in all the blue areas on the reverse side of the design areas you have traced on to tracing paper. Take care not to smudge the crayonned areas so work systematically down the design shapes rather than backwards and forwards. Brush or blow away any specks of dye crayon from the surface of the tracing paper as these could easily spoil your design if they are accidentally left on the paper and then transferred on to the fabric: they would appear as strongly coloured blobs and spots.

5 Before you transfer your designs on to the silky fabric you must make sure that you position the traced designs (waxy side facing towards the fabric) so that they will fall well within the working area of the embroidery frame when the fabric is mounted. Carefully transfer the designs on to the fabric,

ensuring the paper does not slip or move as this will give a smudged and blurred effect.

6 Gently smooth the fabric over the frame on top of the wadding and fix it in place around the sides of the frame. Do not pull it taut as this will flatten the wadding.

7 You are now ready to begin stitching. Use two strands of thread throughout the design. Work from the centre of each design area outwards to the edges. Work tiny Back Stitches along all the outlines of the crazed pattern keeping your stitches neat and even in size.

The flowers are also outlined in Back Stitches with a small cluster of three French Knots in the centre of each open flower surrounded by five small Fly Stitches to give the star-like pattern.

You will find that the wadding flattens quite a lot because of the close stitching but it will retain sufficient puffiness when all the layers are released from the frame and made into the box.

8 When you have completed all the stitchery baste around the edges of the rectangular and circular shapes of quilting. Remove the fabric layers from the frame and trim away the excess fabric leaving at least 1 cm (3/8 in) turning allowance.

9 With right sides together machine Straight Stitch the short ends of the rectangular shape together along the seam line (use the traced pattern to guide you) to form a cylinder shape. Trim away the seam allowance close to the line of machine stitching.

10 Trace on to tracing paper and then cut out the two different sized circles (see page 20) and use these paper patterns as templates.

Using the larger template, cut out an interfacing circle, then use this to cut out a blue silky lining fabric circle allowing an extra 1 cm (3/8 in) around the shape. Place the two circles together, turn the edges of the larger

Trace-off pattern for the sides of the box. The dotted lines represent the seam lines. As the design is split in two here, trace one half then rearrange your tracing paper to trace the second half, accurately matching up the pattern.

silky circle over the edges of the interfacing, folding and pleating the turning neatly to cover the smaller circle. Baste to hold the fabric in position, but do not allow the stitches to show on the right side as these stitches are to remain permanently in place.

With the right side of the cylinder facing outwards fold in a narrow turning to the inside along the lower raw edge (see trace-off pattern for seam line). Baste this to hold in position.

11 With right sides outside place the blue base circle inside the turned edge of the cylinder and with tiny Slip Stitches hand-sew the base and the cylinder together. Make sure that your stitching is very neat and yet very secure and efficient.

12 Using the larger tracing paper template, cut out two more interfacing circles. Cover one of them with another circle of blue lining fabric and cover the second with the quilted lid fabric as in step 10. With right sides outside neatly Slip Stitch the two circles together around their edges.

Cut a long strip of blue fabric to measure 3.5×23 cm (1¼×9 in). Cut another slightly smaller strip of interfacing to measure 1×21 cm (⅜× 8¼ in). Fold the blue strip in half widthwise and, using the interfacing strip as a guide, machine Straight Stitch a seam along the long raw edges of the blue strip. Turn this to the right side (use a safety pin to help you) and then ease the interfacing inside the blue strip so that the seam lies along one of the edges of the interfacing. Tuck one of the raw edges of the blue fabric to the inside of the strip to neaten. Do not bother with the other end at the moment.

With matching thread hand-sew with tiny Slip Stitches, the seamed edge of the strip around the underside of the lid, positioning it 3 mm (⅛ in) in from the edge of the lid. (You can test the position by placing the lid over the box and checking that it fits well.)

When you have worked your way

round to meet the beginning trim the strip if necessary but remember you must leave enough fabric to turn into the open end to neaten. Slip Stitch this join to neaten and complete the rim of the lid.

13 Line the box. Using the smaller of the two tracing paper templates cut out a circle of interfacing and then use this to cut out a blue fabric circle adding a turning allowance of 1 cm (⅜ in) all round. Cover the interfacing circle with the blue fabric as in step 10.

The circle immediately below is the template for the outer base, lid and lid lining. The circle at the foot of the page is the template for the inner lining at the base of the box.

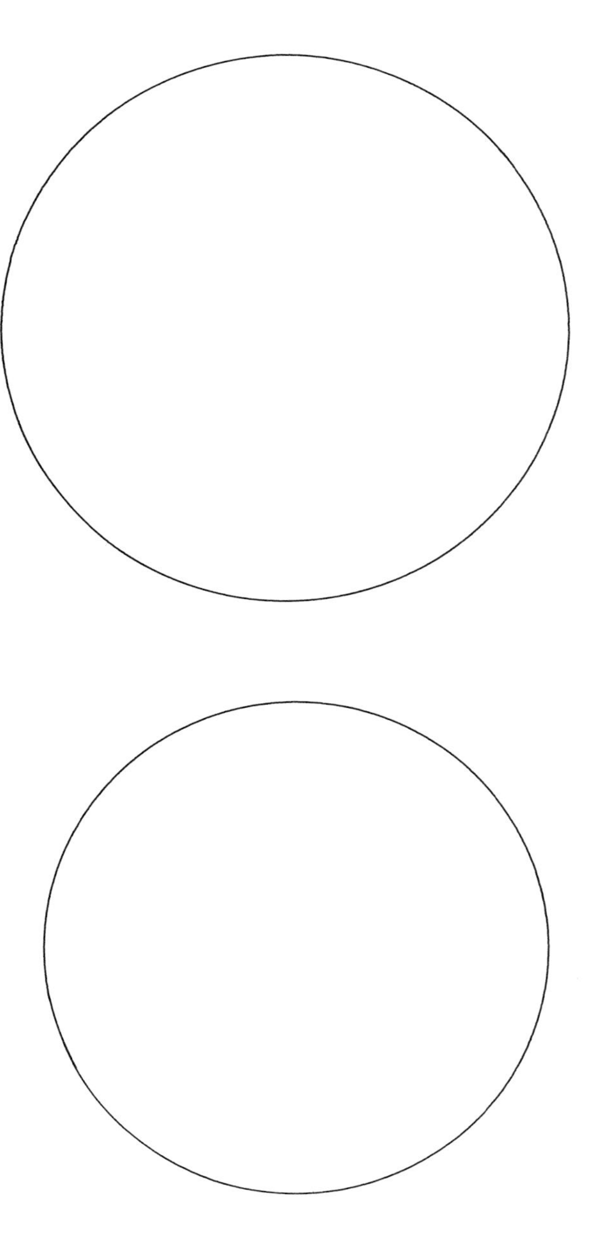

Cut out a rectangular piece of blue fabric to measure 16.5×26.5 cm (6½×10½ in). Make sure that the straight grain of the fabric lies parallel with the sides of the rectangle. With right sides together, machine Straight Stitch the short sides of the rectangle together, working a 1 cm (⅜ in) seam, forming a cylinder. Turn right sides outside and finger-press the seam open and flat. Then turn and finger-press the raw edges of one of the rims inside to the wrong side, allowing only a small turning.

With right sides facing outwards stitch the lining base to the folded edge of the lining cylinder, once more working with tiny Slip Stitches.

Fold a narrow turning to the wrong side around the remaining raw edge of the lining.

14 Turn the quilted box inside out so that the quilting is facing inwards. Fold down to the outside the raw edge or rim of the box so that 2 cm (¾ in) of the embroidery will be on the inside of the box. Baste this turned edge to hold in position. At this point it will be facing you. With the right side of the lining box facing outwards pass this over the wrong side of the quilted box. Match up the seams and pin to hold.

Slip Stitch the folded edge of the lining to the seam line of the quilted fabric.

Turn the box inside out so that the quilting is now on the outside. Push the lining inside the quilting so that the inner base rests on the outer base. Then arrange the lining sides so that they protrude above the quilted sides by approximately 3.5 cm (1¼ in). Finger-press the lining fabric where it folds back on itself and then machine Straight Stitch around this folded edge working 1 cm (⅜ in) away from it.

15 Make a long twisted cord (this will later be cut into three to finish the box). Cut eight equal lengths of Blue Coton Perlé thread, each measuring 3.5 m (3⅞ yd) and use these to make a matching twisted cord (see Special

Techniques, page 138).

16 Using the pointed end of the knitting needle carefully make two holes close to each other in the rim of the channel around the edge of the lining. Ease the knitting needle in through one layer of the channel and gently work the needle backwards and forwards to push the threads of the fabric apart to make a hole rather than by breaking the threads. Then work small Buttonhole Stitches with sewing thread around each hole to neaten them. Make sure the holes are large enough to take the twisted cord.

17 Using a large-eyed needle, thread one end of the twisted cord through the channel. Trim the cord ends near to where they emerge from the lining channel (do not let the cord ends unravel). Then neaten the ends by knotting them and teasing out the threads to make fake tassels. Pull the cord tightly and tie in a neat bow to close the inner lining bag of the quilted box.

18 Hand-sew the remaining twisted cord around the base edge of the box (beginning and ending at the back seam). Neatly secure the cord so that you cannot see the join. Do this by oversewing the cord where it meets and then cut off the excess cord (do not let this length unravel as you need it for the lid) leaving 2.5 cm (1 in) hanging loosely. Unravel the loose ends so that once more they become single strands of Coton Perlé thread then, using a large-eyed needle, neatly pass each thread into the layers of quilting to tidy them away.

19 Finally, sew the remaining length of twisted cord around the edge of the lid and tie the excess into a neat bow. Stitch the bow to hold it in place and then knot the ends of the cord and tease out the raw ends to form mock tassels.

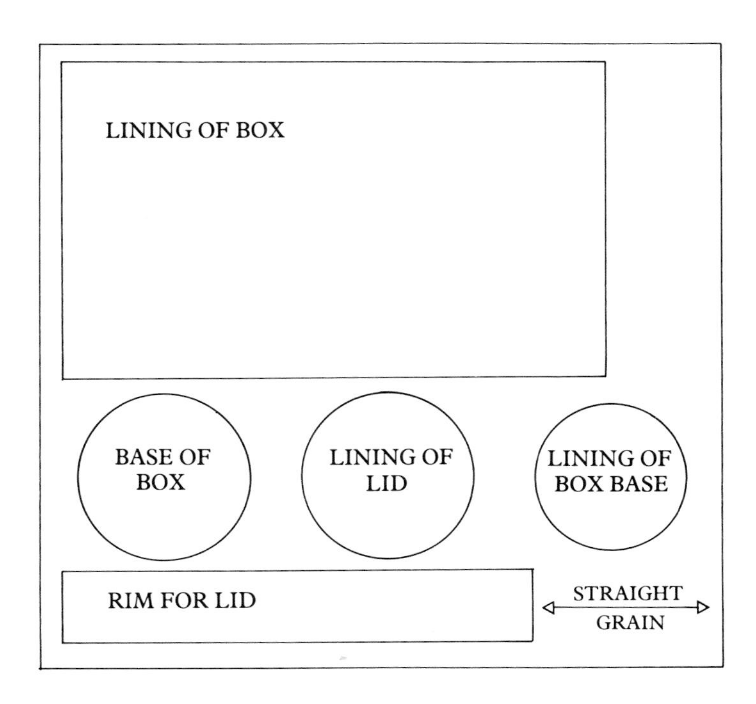

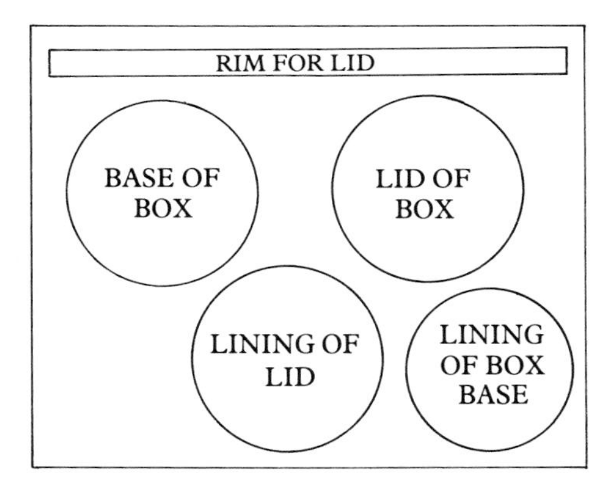

The top cutting plan is for the blue silky fabric. The bottom cutting plan is for the interfacing.

Mandarin Duck Cushion

Using only simple Tent Stitch, this Mandarin Duck design has been worked on canvas and made up as a cushion. It would look equally stunning if framed and mounted on a wall. I have, in fact, also adapted this pattern to make a wall picture, see page 28.

The combination of colours and shapes work well to give a striking design which was inspired by a Chinese silk tapestry weave panel I found in the Victoria & Albert Museum, London. These panels were sewn to the front and back of silk coats worn by Chinese officials in the nineteenth century. In this example the mandarin duck represents a seventh-rank official.

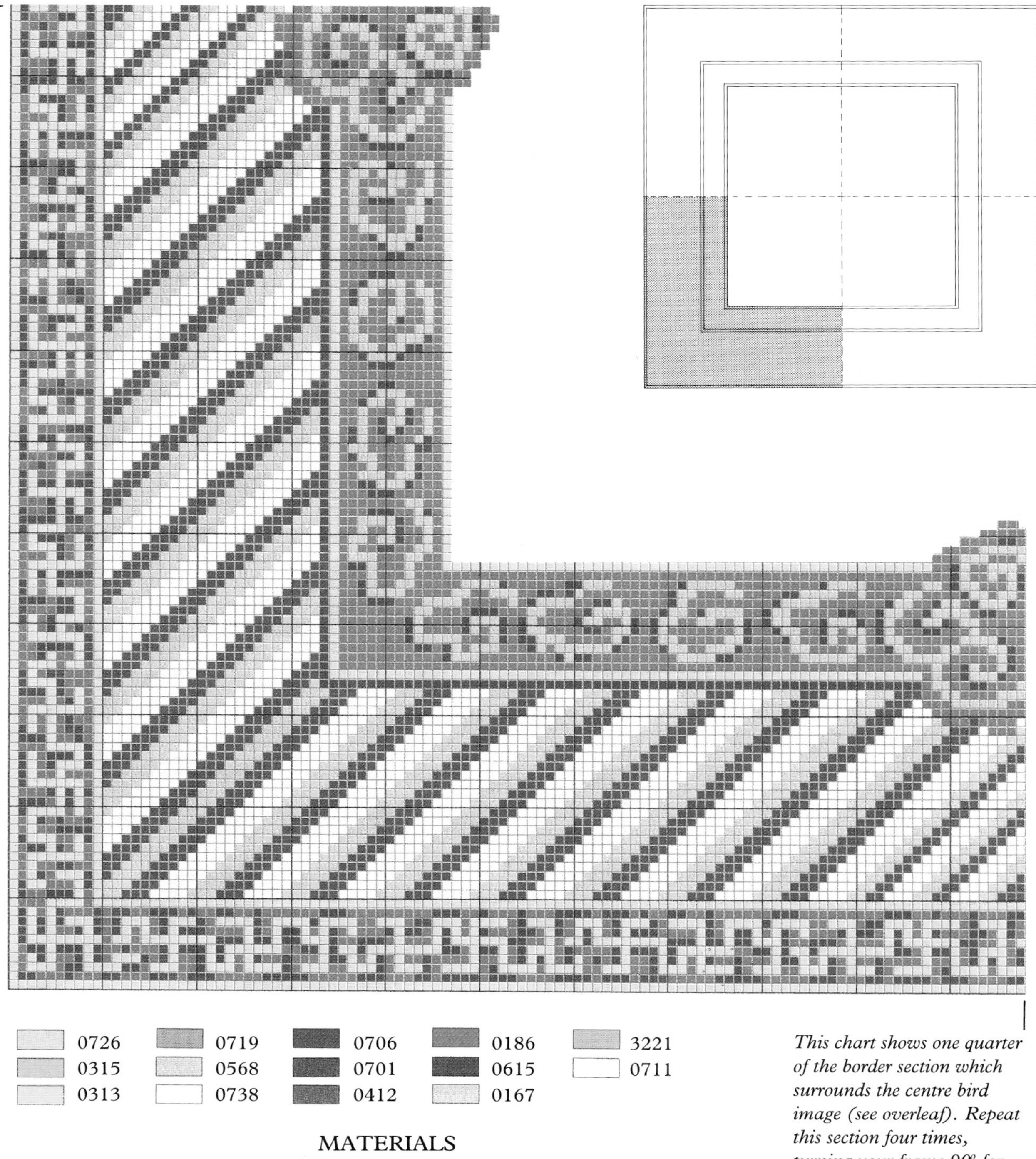

0726	0719	0706	0186	3221
0315	0568	0701	0615	0711
0313	0738	0412	0167	

This chart shows one quarter of the border section which surrounds the centre bird image (see overleaf). Repeat this section four times, turning your frame 90º for each quarter.

MATERIALS

White mono canvas (15 holes per in), 56 cm (22 in) square
Coats tapisserie wool: 6 skeins Turquoise 0186; 5 skeins each Blue 0738, 0568, 0706, Sand 0726; 4 skeins Turquoise 0615; 2 skeins Turquoise 0167; 1 skein each Cream 0711, Rust 0701, 0412, 3221, Orange 0313, 0315, 0719
Turquoise fabric suitable to back cushion, 43 cm (17 in) square
Cushion pad, 40 cm (16 in) square
Sewing thread to match backing fabric
Wooden frame, 50 cm (20 in) square
Waterproof marking pen to mark canvas

Stitches used: *Tent Stitch, machine Straight Stitch, Slip Stitch.*

TO MAKE THE CUSHION

1 Stretch the canvas on the frame, ensuring the threads are parallel to the sides of the frame.

2 Find the centre of the canvas by counting the threads. Then lightly mark the horizontal and vertical centre guidelines to establish the centre of the canvas (the centre point is a hole and not an intersection of threads). Each square of the chart represents one Tent Stitch, which in turn is worked over one horizontal and one vertical thread of canvas.

It does not really matter where you start your stitchery. You can start in the centre and work outwards or you may find it satisfying and helpful to count carefully along one of the guidelines and begin by working the turquoise border with the scrolled shapes and then building up the centre area and the outer bands. Generally, you will find it easier to work from the centre or near centre outwards. When working the narrow outer band of the design work the sand-coloured pattern first and then fill in the turquoise background quite randomly to give a speckled and broken effect.

Use your yarn as economically as possible and always begin and finish off the yarn ends securely. Never jump across the wrong side of the canvas from one area to another, but finish off and start again. Also do not use very long lengths of yarn as the action of passing the soft woollen yarn backwards and forwards through the holes of the canvas will gradually wear it thin. Never attempt to work a stitch in one single move, this will strain the

This is the centre section of the cushion showing the mandarin duck design. It is surrounded by the border (see the chart on the previous page).

canvas and distort the stitchery as an uneven tension is likely to be the result (working within a frame encourages good and even stitchery).

3 Follow the chart accurately and gradually build up the design. Check frequently that you have not made any errors as it is easy to count one square or stitch too many or too few. If a mistake is made remember that with a little patience you can unpick the stitches in question and re-work them correctly.

4 Once you have completed the entire design remove the canvas from the frame and trim away the excess, leaving a 1 cm (⅜ in) seam allowance on all sides. With right sides facing, pin and then baste and machine Straight Stitch the cushion face and back together along the edge of the canvaswork stitchery. Remember to leave an opening along one side to push the cushion pad in. Carefully clip across the seam allowance at the corners. Turn to the right side and fill with the cushion pad.

Fold in the seam allowance along the opening and Slip Stitch the folded edges together to close.

0726 0719 0706 0186 3221
0315 0568 0701 0615 0711
0313 0738 0412 0167

If you are worried about working the larger cushion you might prefer to start on the smaller wall picture (see the instructions and chart overleaf).

Mandarin Duck Wall Picture

This delightful design has been adapted from the Mandarin Duck cushion. It is a simplified version of the original Chinese panel and looks stunning as a wall picture placed within a carefully chosen picture frame.

MATERIALS

White mono canvas (15 holes per in), 25 × 30 cm (10 × 12 in) square
Coats tapisserie wool: 1 skein each Blue 0706, 0568, 0738, Cream 0711, Sand 0726, Orange 0313, 0315, 0719, Rust 0412, 0701, 3221, Turquoise 0615, 0186, 0167
Firm cardboard to stretch canvas upon, 23 × 17 cm (9 × 7 in)
Strong yarn or string to lace canvas on cardboard
Picture frame
Wooden frame, 25 × 30 cm (10 × 12 in)
Waterproof marking pen to mark canvas

Stitches used: *Tent Stitch.*

NB. If you have worked the Mandarin Duck cushion then you will find that you will have some yarns left over from this project. You will probably have enough of most of the colours to work one of these wall pictures but you will need to have a full skein of the three Blue shades 0738, 0568, 0706, and Sand 0726.

TO WORK THE PICTURE

1 Stretch the canvas on the small frame, ensuring the threads are parallel to the sides of the frame. You will find that the canvas is not large enough to fold around the sides of the frame but staple or tack it onto the 'top' surface of the frame. This reduces the amount of wastage of canvas around the edges of the canvaswork.

2 Find and mark the centre guidelines of the design and then commence working following the chart accurately. Read the advice given in step 2 of the cushion design (see page 24) before starting.

When you have completed the design, remove it from the frame and stretch it tightly over the piece of firm cardboard, lacing it with the strong yarn or string (see Special Techniques page 140).

3 Finally, select a frame to mount the canvaswork within. Your frame should enhance the rich colours of the design and show off the texture of the canvaswork. If you place the work behind glass it will be preserved from dust but a certain richness will be lost.

0726
0315
0313
0719
0568
0738
0706
0701
0412
0186
0615
0167
3221
0711

Butterflies Trinket Box

A little time, patience and accuracy is required for this delightful box. But if you don't want to tackle the whole project remember you can use the motifs for other items. They would look stunning if worked along the borders of towels or individually on bed linen and perhaps a nightdress. They could also be worked on table linen and tray cloths; the motifs are ready for you to adapt.

I worked this project on an inexpensive synthetic fabric but its rich appearance makes it look like pure silk. The embroidery gives a dense and jewel-like effect yet only simple stitches such as Satin Stitch, Back Stitch and French Knots have been used.

To enrich the box further I added a twisted cord. This not only embellishes the total design but also hides the stitches that can be seen once the box has been constructed.

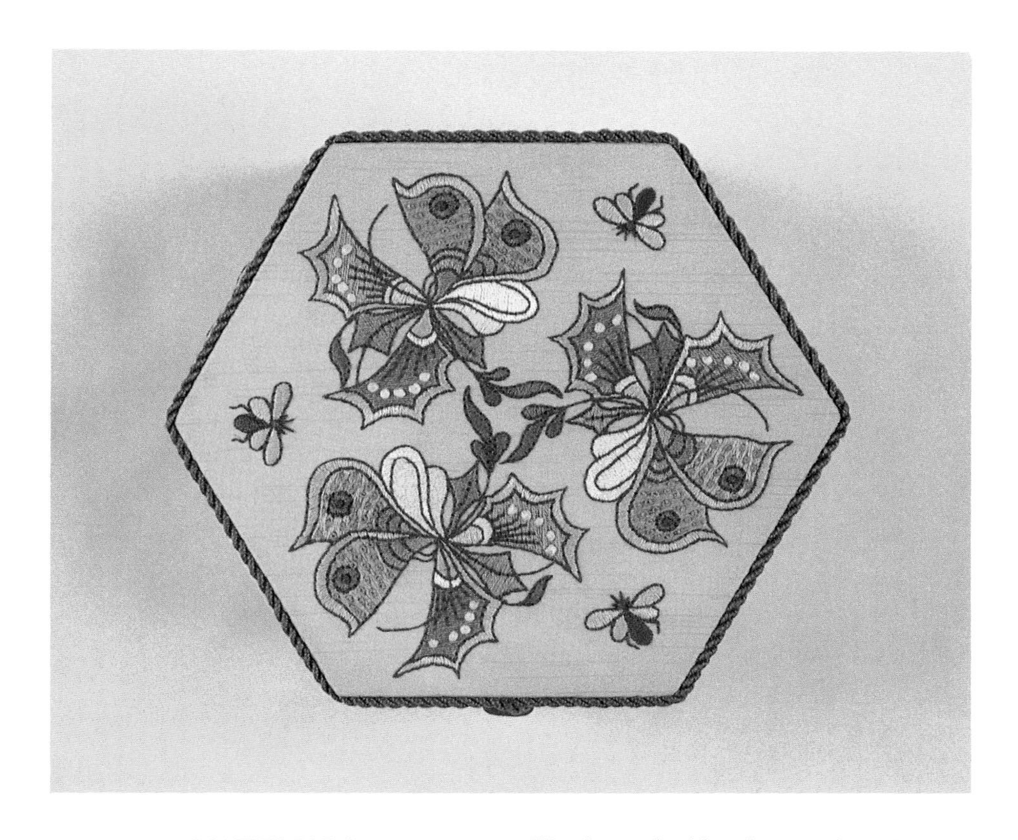

This shows the arrangement of the butterflies on the lid. To work these see the trace-off pattern overleaf.

MATERIALS

Duck-egg-blue, silky-type synthetic fabric, 40 × 50 cm (16 × 20 in)
White cotton backing fabric, 20 × 70 cm (8 × 28 in)
Emerald-green, silky-type synthetic fabric, 30 × 80 cm (12 × 31 in)
Pelmet or heavyweight interfacing (Vilene), 15 × 30 cm (6 × 12 in)
Firm cardboard, 30 × 35 cm (12 × 14 in)
Coats Anchor stranded embroidery thread, 2 skeins Plum 972; 1 skein each Mauve 86, 95, Green 185, 187, 204, 206, Yellow 275, 292, 301
Coats Coton Perlé No. 5, 1 skein Green 187
Sewing thread to match silky-type fabrics
Basting thread
Masking tape
1 Easy-Cover button, 12 mm (½ in) diameter
Green- or blue-coloured crayon
Sharp craft knife
Ruler
Cutting mat or board
Wooden embroidery hoop, 15 or 18 cm (6 or 7 in) diameter
Small rotating frame
Tracing paper

Stitches used: *Diagonal Basting Stitch, Satin Stitch, Back Stitch, French Knots, Slip Stitch, Running Stitch.*

TO WORK THE LID AND SIDES

1 Referring to the cutting plan on page 35 cut out the pieces for the lid and sides from the duck-egg-blue, silky fabric. Reserve the remaining fabric to be used for the underside of the base.

Also cut out the white cotton backing pieces.

2 Stretch the lid piece of the silky fabric centrally in the wooden hoop and place it flat against the trace-off pattern (see page 32). Use the coloured crayon to trace the butterfly design directly on to the fabric. Make sure the crayon has a sharp point so that the lines are as fine as possible. Remove the fabric from the hoop and

Trace-off pattern for the lid. When tracing the design for your embroidery do not draw the outer hexagon shape. This is to be used for the template when making the box (see Step 1 opposite).

place it right side upwards over the cotton backing shape. Stretch the two layers carefully within the hoop ensuring they are both smooth and taut. The lid is now ready to embroider.

3 Trace the side shapes (see page 33) on to a strip of tracing paper, repeating them until you have six alternating sides with a small gap in between each side. Tape this on to a smooth flat (preferably white) surface then tape the long strip of silky fabric centrally over the tracing and once more carefully and accurately trace the butterflies and insects on to the fabric using the coloured crayon. Release the fabric and the tracing paper strips. Reserve the trace-off pattern.

Place the fabric strip right side upwards over the backing fabric and, using Diagonal Basting Stitches (see Special Techniques page 137) baste the two strips together. Carefully mount the strip in the rotating frame. The side strip is now ready to embroider.

4 Use two strands of embroidery thread at all times. You will find it neater and more effective if you fill in all the areas of the design in Satin Stitches before working the outlines of Back Stitches.

Follow the colour plans of the butterflies. The three on the lid are all worked to the same scheme as are those around the sides. You can choose to follow the colour scheme of the small insects shown here or vary them if you wish. The areas of Satin Stitches are all worked across the width of the various shapes rather than along their length. This gives a more tightly controlled effect.

Once you have worked all the shapes in Satin Stitches then you can add the French Knots as shown on the colour plans and finally work the tiny outline Back Stitches to complete the embroidery.

TO MAKE THE BOX

1 Trace and cut out from the tracing paper a hexagonal template.

Using the sharp craft knife, ruler and the cutting mat or board cut out two cardboard hexagons. One must be identical to the template, to be used for the base; the other needs to be very slightly bigger, to be made into the lid. Then cut out six cardboard rectangles of identical size using the side template (use the trace-off pattern below to help you).

2 Cut out two hexagon shapes and one long strip from the lining fabric (see the cutting plan on page 35). Remember to add 1 cm (⅜ in) seam allowance all round the hexagon shapes.

3 Cover the base.
Cut out a hexagon shape plus 1 cm (⅜ in) seam allowance all round using the remaining piece of light turquoise fabric for the underside of the base.

With the right side of the turquoise fabric facing down on a clean, flat surface place the smaller card hexagon centrally over it and pin the fabric shape around the edges of the card. Pin into the cut edge of the card (see the illustration above). Stretch the fabric smoothly against the cardboard. Fold the turning allowance to the wrong side of the cardboard and use masking tape to hold the turned fabric in position snipping away the excess fabric at each corner to cover the cardboard shape neatly.

Finger-press the masking tape firmly to the cardboard to hold.

Cut out an interfacing hexagon shape and cover with one of the lining pieces turning the seam allowance around the edges of the interfacing and basting it to hold. Do not allow your stitches to pass through to the right side of the covered shape as these stitches will remain permanently in position.

With wrong sides together and using matching thread, Slip Stitch the two base shapes together working very small, neat stitches around the edges of the hexagonal shape.

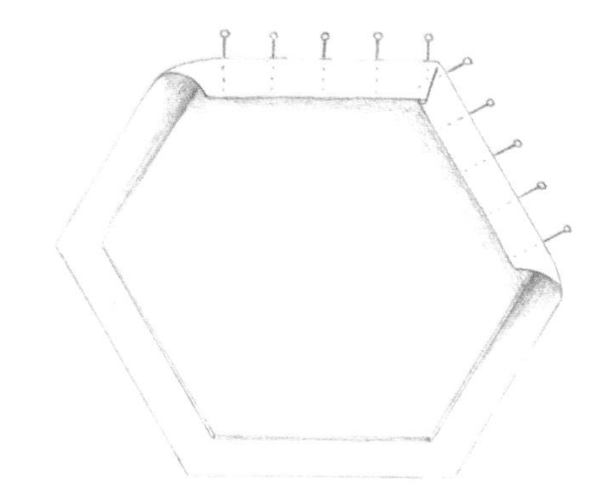

With right sides facing downwards, carefully stretch the embroidered fabric over and around the slightly larger cardboard hexagon. Push dressmakers' pins through the fabric and into the cut edge of the cardboard to hold in place.

Trace-off pattern for the sides of the box. Repeat these, alternating them to produce a continuous strip of six sides (three of each design motif). The small gap between each side is to allow for the 'angle' of each corner when making the box. They must therefore be allowed for when transferring the designs on to the fabric. Do not trace the dotted lines on to the fabric.

4 Make the lid.
Repeat the process above (using the embroidered lid instead of turquoise fabric) to cover the lid which is very slightly larger. Remember to cut the heavyweight interfacing to match the size of the cardboard hexagon shape.
5 Make the sides of the box.
Use the trace-off pattern from step 3 of making the lid and sides to help you. Cut out the embroidered strip allowing a 1 cm (3/8 in) turning allowance on all sides.

Cut out the emerald-green lining strip, 7×80 cm (2¾×31 in). Turn a narrow allowance to the wrong side of the strip along both of the long sides, pinch fold them and then with matching sewing thread work a line of tiny Running/Gathering Stitches close to each folded edge. Do not secure or fasten off the threads. Leave them loose so you can pull them to gather the strip of fabric.

With the wrong side of the embroidered strip facing down on a clean, flat surface, carefully and accurately place the six card sections in position. The trace-off pattern will be of great help. (Remember to leave a gap between each section as shown on the pattern.)

Using dressmaker's pins and then masking tape fix the turning allowance of the fabric strip securely to the wrong side of the cardboard sections. Fold the short ends very neatly and fix them in place on the wrong side of the cardboard.

You can see the lining fabric inside the box has been gathered to finish the sides neatly.

With wrong sides together join the short ends of the covered card strip to those of the lining strip. Then gently pull the gathering threads, evenly dispersing the tiny folds of lining fabric along the entire length of the strip. With a double length of sewing thread stitch the gathered edges of the lining fabric to the taped edges of the embroidered fabric.

Join the short ends of the embroidered strip together to form the outer sides of the hexagon box. Similarly, join the short ends of the inner gathered sides together. Use a double length of thread to do this, working small, neat stitches.

Pin the sides to the base, digging the pins in at the corners of the hexagon shape to hold them together. Stitch the sides to the base with double thread and small stitches. The sides should sit neatly on top of the base overlapping it very slightly.
6 Place the lid on top of the box and decide which position is best (depending on your accuracy of cutting and making-up you may find a slight difference in the lid and the sides.

Stitch one of the six edges of the hexagon lid shape to the top edge of the box sides to coincide with the position of the join in the sides which is the back of the box. Once more, use a double length of thread for extra strength and work tiny, closely-spaced stitches. I find that with this sort of process a thimble is of great assistance and it certainly saves your fingers from too much hard work!
7 Make a twisted cord using the skein of green Coton Perlé. Unravel the skein and divide it evenly into four lengths. You will have to do this carefully or the lengths will become muddled; ask someone to help you if

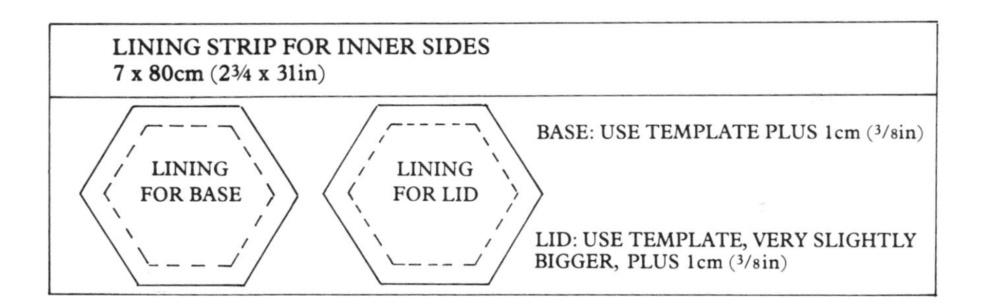

possible. Use the four lengths to make a long, twisted cord (see Special Techniques page 138).

8 Cover the Easy-Cover button with a small piece of the emerald-green lining fabric, following the manufacturer's instructions. Securely stitch this in position near the top and at the centre of the box side directly opposite the back of the box.

9 Stitch the cord around the edges of the base of the box. Begin and end with about 2.5 cm (1 in) to spare. Use a small piece of masking tape to prevent the cut ends of the cord from unravelling.

Stitch the remaining length of twisted cord around the top rim of the box sides and then around the edges of the lid. Start and end at one corner at the back of the box where the lid is attached. Then you can pass the cord from the rim of the sides straight on to the lid edge attaching it all in one length without having to cut the cord.

Twist the cord into a small loop to form a button loop at the centre front of the lid to coincide with the position of the button on the front side of the box.

10 Neaten all the cord ends using a large-eyed needle, as follows. Unravel the twisted cord ends so that each cord reverts back to groups of the much thinner Coton Perlé threads. Pass each individual thread into the side or base of the box and then carefully bring the needle out to the surface and trim the thread end pulling it so that once cut it slips back into the layers of fabric and is hidden from sight.

BACKING STRIP FOR SIDES
20 x 50cm (8 x 20cm)

BACKING FOR LID
20cm (8in) SQUARE

STRIP FOR EMBROIDERED SIDES OF BOX
20 x 50cm (8 x 20cm)

EMBROIDERED LID OF BOX
20cm (8in) SQUARE

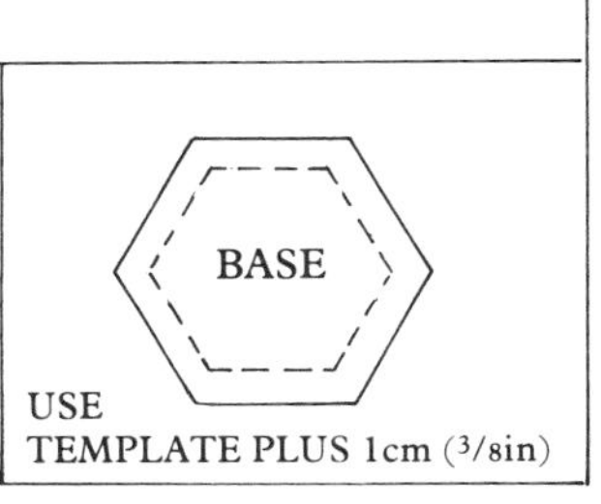

USE TEMPLATE PLUS 1cm (3/8in)

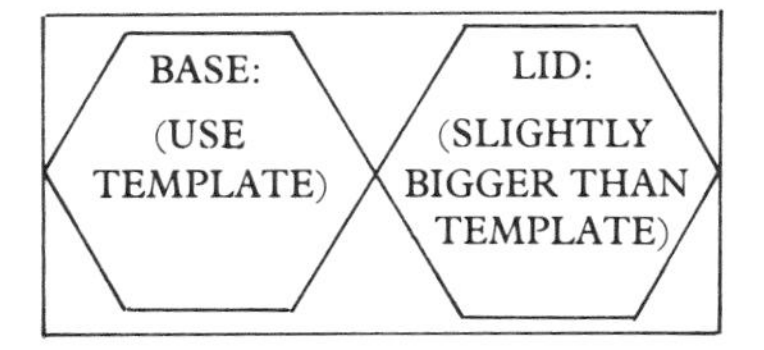

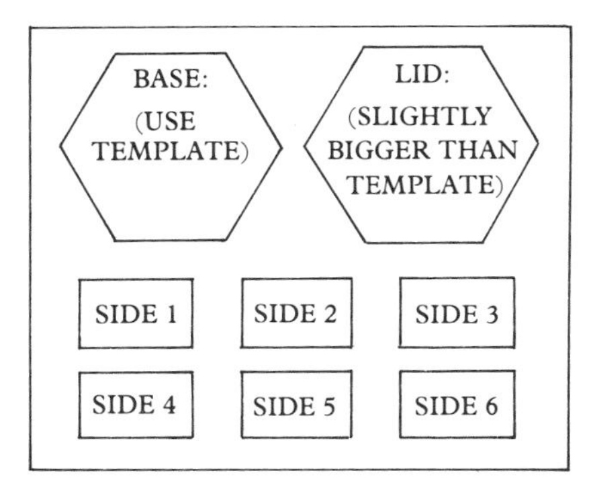

Cutting plans for (from top to bottom): emerald silky-type fabric, white cotton backing fabric, duck-egg-blue silky-type fabric, heavyweight (pelmet) interfacing, firm cardboard.

Precious Pillow

The rich colouring, detailed stitchery and fine silk fabric all contribute towards the effect of this charming pillow. I have used a combination of stranded and Coton Perlé threads to emphasize different parts of the design in different ways. For example, the smooth and even effect that I achieved by working Satin Stitches in stranded thread is used for parts of the birds' bodies while, in contrast, I worked the long narrow bands that border each design section in Couching Stitch, using softly twisted Coton Perlé thread.

The rich and precious effect was achieved primarily through the choice of fabrics and threads but remember you can easily alter this effect by experimenting with and changing your selection of materials. For instance, a totally different but equally successful pillow could be created by using a coarser fabric and non-shiny yarns such as crewel wools or matt cotton threads such as 'Nordin' yarns. For a complete change in interpretation simply place your trace-off pattern under some canvas and trace the design on to the surface of the canvas with a waterproof marking pen. Then select your shades of tapestry wool and work either with a variety of stitches or entirely in Tent Stitch.

I have worked the bands of design diagonally but you could use them horizontally, if you prefer.

MATERIALS

White silk fabric (with slight slub), 35 × 70 cm (14 × 28 in)

White cotton fabric to back embroidery, 35 × 70 cm (14 × 28 in)

White cotton fabric to line pillow, 23 × 44 cm (9 × 17¼ in)

Coats Anchor stranded embroidery thread: 2 skeins each Rust 13, Gold 306, Blue 132; 1 skein Light Gold 301

Coats Coton Perlé thread: 1 skein each Rust 340, Gold 306, Blue 132, Light Gold 305

White sewing thread

Basting thread

Small amount of terylene or polyester filling
Small amount of pot pourri
Good-quality tracing paper
Black fine-tipped felt pen
Clear adhesive tape
Blue and orange crayons
Embroidery frame, 30 cm (12 in) square

Stitches used: *Couching Stitch, French Knots, Running Stitch, Back Stitch, Straight Stitch, Satin Stitch, Slip Stitch, machine Straight Stitch.*

TO MAKE THE PRECIOUS PILLOW

1 Press your fabrics to remove any creases. Cut the white silk fabric into two equal pieces each measuring 35 cm (14 in) square. Do the same with the larger piece of white cotton fabric. Reserve a square of silk and of cotton fabric to be used for the reverse side of the pillow.

2 Stretch the remaining cotton square on the embroidery frame, ensuring that the grain of the fabric is parallel with the sides of the frame.

3 Make an accurate tracing of the pillow design (see above) using the felt pen and the tracing paper. Then temporarily fix it on to a clean, flat surface; ideally this should be white, if not place a sheet of white paper underneath the tracing paper to make the design show up clearly.

Tape the silk square centrally over the traced design, stretching the fabric slightly as you fix it securely to the working surface. It should be smooth and taut. The grain of the fabric should be parallel to the dotted lines of the traced design which represent the seam line of the pillow.

Using the blue and orange crayons, carefully and accurately trace the design on to the silk fabric. Keep the tips of the crayons as fine and as sharp as possible so that your drawn lines will be easily concealed by the stitchery. (Do not trace the dotted seam line. The scallop shapes within the birds' wings and the speckles on their bodies may also be omitted if you are confident enough to work them freely by eye.)

Once you have completed the

305 *Coton Perlé couched with 301 stranded*
301 *stranded*
306 *Coton Perlé couched with 306 stranded*
306 *stranded*
132 *stranded*
13 *stranded*
340 *Coton Perlé couched with 13 stranded*

Opposite, Different textures have been achieved by using a combination of Coton Perlé and stranded threads on the pure silk fabric.

tracing release the silk fabric and reserve the trace-off pattern. Stretch the silk fabric on the frame aligning the silk grain with the sides of the frame.

4 Before you begin your embroidery measure, cut and carefully reserve eight 150-cm (60-in) lengths of Rust and Blue Coton Perlé thread to be used to make the twisted cord (step 16).

5 It does not really matter where you begin your embroidery but you may find it helpful to work the narrow bands that border each of the different sections of the design.

When using the stranded embroidery thread use three strands at a time, but use a single or double length of Coton Perlé thread according to the instructions.

6 Gold-coloured bands:
Each band is built up of three rows of gold-coloured Couching Stitch, using stranded thread to hold in position a double length of Coton Perlé thread per row. Simply work a small stitch at right angles across the Coton Perlé, ensuring that the stitches are neatly and evenly spaced and that the Coton Perlé lies in a straight line, following your traced design. When you work the second row place your stitches across the thicker threads so that they lie centrally between the stitches of the first row, then work the stitches along the third row so that they are in line with those of the first row. This creates a neat basketweave or brick pattern.

Using the trace-off pattern and the photograph (see opposite) for reference, work a single line of Rust couching along the sides of the golden bands, aligning the tiny holding stitches of Rust stranded thread with those already worked and using only a single length of Rust Coton Perlé per row.

7 Spiral bands:
Using Light Gold stranded thread, catch a double length of Coton Perlé thread over the traced spiral shapes of these rows.

8 Blue and gold bands:
Using Blue stranded thread and working in evenly and closely spaced Satin Stitches, completely fill in the background area of these bands by working your stitches parallel to one short side of the small triangles that divide the background area. Then fill in the next triangle so that the stitches lie in the opposite direction (at right angles to those of the previous set). Continue in this way until each band is completely filled with stitchery.

Then work over the blue triangles with Gold Coton Perlé thread. Use a single length and work five evenly spaced Straight Stitches across each blue triangle, placing the stitches so that they lie at right angles to the Satin Stitches below them.

9 Birds and plants bands:
These are worked entirely in stranded thread. If you look at the main photograph you will see that there are two alternating variations to the way the pairs of birds are worked, although the method is the same.

Outline the shape of the birds and work their legs and feet in small neat Back Stitches using Rust thread. Using the same colour work the tiny Running Stitches which represent the speckles on the birds with white chests. Also work a single French Knot for the eye of each bird. Then build up in Back Stitch the minute scallop shapes which represent the feathers of the wings which are white.

Using Gold thread work close and even Satin Stitches across the width of the remaining wings and then complete them by working the tiny Back Stitch scallop pattern as before.

Using Light Gold thread, work close and even Satin Stitches across the bodies of the birds (refer to the photograph to see which ones are coloured). Work your Satin Stitches from the inner edge of the wing to the outer edge of the body and make sure your stitching does not cover the French Knot eye.

The plants are all worked in the same way. The stem is simply a line of Blue Back Stitches. Then work the blue leaves in closely spaced Satin Stitches to give gracefully curved shapes, using the photograph to guide you. It does not matter if the leaves vary a little from one plant to the next as this adds interest to the finished embroidery.

Work the remaining leaves in the same way using Gold thread and then work the head of the plant with the Satin Stitches radiating out from the stem.

Finally, work Rust Back Stitches along the upper half of the stem to add a slight shadow effect. Use the same thread and stitch to work along the upper edges of three of the Gold leaves (refer to the photograph). Then add several Rust Straight Stitches radiating out from each plant head.

10 When your embroidery is complete remove the fabric from the frame and reserve it safely in a clean, flat place while you work the reverse side of the pillow. You do not have to work embroidery on the back of the pillow but it adds a charming touch to include a pair of birds on the reverse.

Stretch the reserved cotton fabric square on the frame. Trace the bottom right-hand pair of birds from the traced paper pattern on to the silk fabric in the same way as you traced the complete design (see step 4). Then stretch the silk on to the frame.

11 Embroider the pair of birds in the same way as on the pillow front (you can choose which variation of colours your prefer). When you have completed your embroidery remove the fabric from the frame.

12 Place the pillow front facing upwards, on a clean flat surface.

Trim around the seam line of your reserved trace-off pattern and place this on top of the embroidery, aligning the traced shapes with the stitched shapes below. Using a small piece of clear adhesive tape hold the pattern in position and trim away the excess fabric, leaving a 1 cm (3/8 in) seam allowance all around. Lift the tracing paper off the fabric and repeat the process with the pillow back.

13 With right sides facing, very carefully pin and baste the pillow front and back together. Once more you will find it helpful to use the trace-off pattern to align the layers accurately. Baste around the seam line. Set your sewing machine to Straight Stitch and, using white sewing thread, machine around the seam line, leaving an opening along one side of approximately 10 cm (4 in).

Clip the surplus fabric away across the corners before turning the pillow to the right side. Ease out the corner points without damaging the fabric.

14 Make the pillow lining. Fold the remaining piece of white cotton fabric in half and machine stitch around the three open sides with a 1 cm (3/8 in) seam allowance. Leave an opening.

Clip across the corners to remove surplus fabric and turn the pillow lining to the right side. Fill it with a combination of pot pourri and terylene or polyester filling. Turn in the raw edges and close the opening with neat hand stitches.

15 Place the pillow inside the embroidered cover and close the opening.

16 Finally, make a two-colour twisted cord using the reserved cut lengths of Coton Perlé thread (see Special Techniques page 138). With two strands of Blue or Rust thread carefully Slip Stitch the cord around the seam line of the pillow so that the loose ends of cord meet at the bottom right-hand corner. Trim the cord ends to approximately 5 cm (2 in) then knot the cord carefully before you cut it or it will unravel. Tease out the cut threads beyond the knots to make fluffy mock tassels.

Fish and Waterlily Bath Linen

A richly embroidered border can turn a plain towel into something very special with which to greet a guest. These towels with their borders of fish and water-lillies will certainly make them feel welcome.

I have worked the border of the peach-coloured towel heavily with lots of Satin Stitches and Chain Stitches among others. In stark contrast the inky-blue towel border has only simple outlines of the same design worked in Back Stitches, with just some French Knots added for the fishes' eyes. As you will appreciate, the inky-blue border can be worked speedily and simply while the peachy border requires some skill and patient devotion.

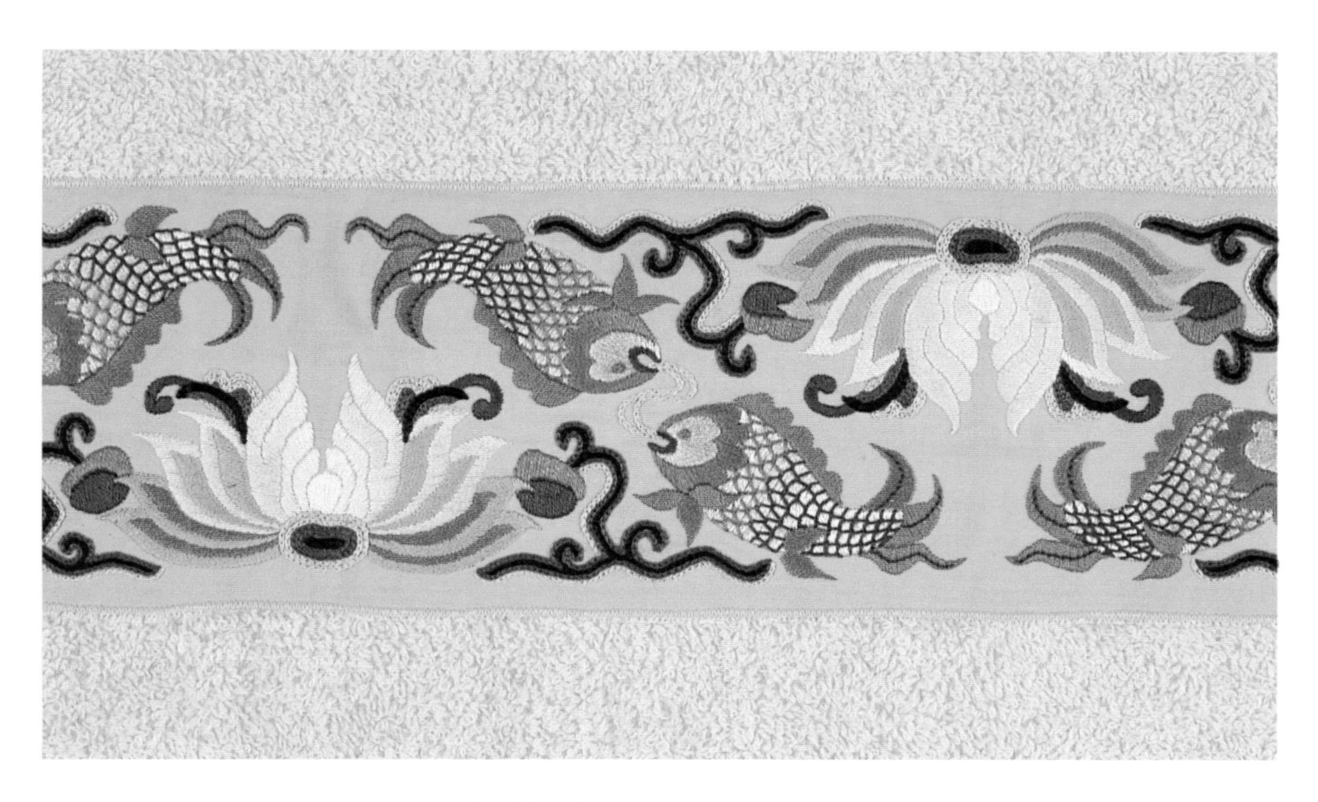

MATERIALS

(for the peach-coloured towel)

Peach cotton fabric, 25 × 66 cm (10 × 26 in)
White cotton backing fabric, 25 × 66 cm (10 × 26 in)
Peach hand towel, approximately 56 cm (22 in) wide
Coats Anchor stranded thread: 2 skeins each Pink 11, Blue 175; 1 skein each Pink 24, 271, Blue 119, 120, Cream 275, Green 246, 253, 267
Peach sewing thread
Basting thread
Small rotating frame or wooden embroidery hoop, 20 cm (8 in) diameter
Fabric transfer pencil or dark-peach-coloured crayon
Tracing paper

Stitches used: *Diagonal Basting Stitch, Chain Stitch, Satin Stitch, Fly Stitch, French Knots, Back Stitch, Slip Stitch, machine Satin Stitch.*

To work this richly embroidered border follow the trace-off pattern and instructions overleaf.

Trace-off pattern for both borders. The simpler Back Stitch version (see page 45) is shown on the right. The heavily embroidered version is shown on the left (follow the direction shown for all the Satin Stitch areas for the best effect). Use the instructions and the drawing above to help you work either version. For extra help see the close-ups on pages 41 and 45.

TO WORK THE PEACH BORDER

1 Trace the fish and waterlily design above on to a strip of tracing paper, repeating it as many times as necessary to equal the width of your hand towel. If using a fabric transfer pencil then carefully draw over all the design lines on the reverse side of the tracing paper. Make sure the point of the pencil is kept sharp so that you will get a fine and accurate mark. (Test the pencil on a spare piece of fabric if you are unfamiliar with this technique, also see page 135). Follow the manufacturer's instructions carefully to transfer the design on to the strip of fabric.

If you use a coloured crayon the easiest way is probably to fix temporarily the traced design on to a window and then fix the peach fabric (free of any creases) centrally over the tracing paper. Then simply transfer the design on to the fabric. Once more, a fine point to the crayon will ensure only fine lines are drawn on to the fabric.

2 Place your peach fabric, right side uppermost, over the strip of white backing fabric and align their edges. Smooth the two layers together and work lines of Diagonal Basting Stitches along the strip to keep the layers together (see Special Techniques page 137).

Mount the short ends of the strip upon the rotating ends of the frame. Alternatively stretch one end of the strip in your hoop, gently pulling the fabric around the hoop to give a taut working area within it. You will have to adjust the position of the fabric within both the hoop and the frame as you progress along the embroidered border strip.

3 You are now ready to begin your embroidery. Use two strands of thread at all times, to give a very fine and detailed effect. Refer to the colour plan above to help you when selecting the colour of thread.

All the green areas are worked in very small lines of Chain Stitches. Work the solid areas so that you grade

the colours from light green through mid-green to dark green (see the colour plan).

The remaining areas of the design, the fish and waterlily flowers, are worked in closely-spaced areas of Satin Stitches which give a beautifully rich yet smooth effect to contrast with the Chain Stitches.

To embellish the fish bodies work a lacy pattern of a variation of Fly Stitch. Instead of working isolated Fly Stitches work them in rows rather like step-ladders so that you gradually cover the main body shape of each fish (see the illustration on page 42). Work the tail end of the shape in dark blue and then gradually change to the mid-blue at the head end.

Finally work a single dark pink French Knot for the eye and work neat lines of Back Stitches in dark blue centrally along the tail fins to complete. Reposition the fabric within the frame or hoop and work the next section of the border. Continue until finished.

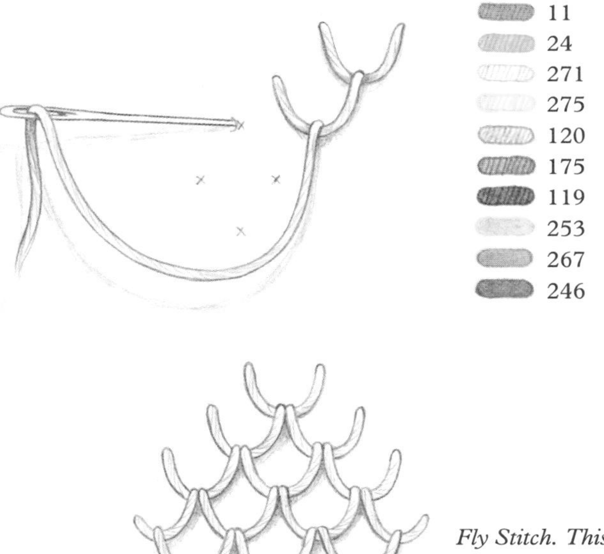

Fly Stitch. This is used to represent the fish's body on the peach colourway. Start at the tail end with a single Fly Stitch then work in a slanting direction gradually building up lines of the stitch. As you work, change the thread colour from dark blue to mid-blue towards the head.

4 When you have completed the embroidery remove the fabric from the frame or hoop and if necessary press it carefully on the wrong side to remove any creases.

Use the tracing paper design strip to mark the edges of the border. Trim each edge of the strip accurately along the straight lines. Then, aligning the traced design with its embroidered counterpart, lightly mark the border with a coloured crayon. Accurately cut away the excess fabric on each edge.

Pin and baste the border across one end of the towel, tucking in the turned allowance at both short ends, trim a little of the fabric away if necessary. Using matching sewing thread, attach the strip securely to the towel with machine Satin Stitch along the raw edges of the border, covering them completely with the width of the Satin Stitches.

5 Finally, Slip Stitch the turned allowance to the towel sides to neaten and finish this project.

MATERIALS

(for the inky-blue towel)

Inky-blue cotton fabric, 25 × 66 cm (10 × 26 in)
White cotton backing fabric, 25 × 66 cm (10 × 26 in)
Inky-blue hand towel, approximately 56 cm (22 in) wide
Coats Anchor stranded thread, 1 skein each Pink 11, 24, 271, Blue 119, 120, 175, Cream 275, Green 253, 267
Inky-blue sewing thread
Basting thread
Small rotating frame or wooden embroidery hoop, 20 cm (8 in) diameter
Fabric transfer pencil (light-coloured) or white crayon
Light-coloured or white dressmaker's carbon paper
Tracing paper

This version is easily and quickly worked in Back Stitch and French Knots.

TO WORK THE INKY-BLUE BORDER

1 Use the same design as the peach border and trace it on to a long strip of tracing paper. Choose your method to transfer the design along the centre of the inky-blue fabric.

You may find it difficult to trace through the fabric because of its dark colour but if you work against a well-lit window it can be done.

Alternatively use a light-coloured transfer pencil or white dressmaker's carbon paper, following the manufacturer's instructions.

You will probably have a preference for a particular method of transferring designs on to fabric. I personally prefer tracing directly on to fabric with a suitably coloured crayon as it is quick and accurate and does not smudge or blur.

2 Once you have transferred your design on to the fabric prepare it together with the backing fabric within the frame or hoop (see step 2 of the peach border on page 42).

3 The stitchery for this version of the design is quick and easy. Simply work along all the lines of the design in Back Stitches using three strands of thread and then work a French Knot for each fish's eyes (follow the colour plan on page 43).

4 When the border is complete remove the fabric from the frame and make up in the same way as the peach towel (see steps 4 and 5 opposite).

If you want to make a set of towels simply measure the width of the towels and make your borders to match, allowing a little extra for the turning allowances.

Bamboo Evening Purse and Handkerchiefs

The elegant simplicity of this evening purse was inspired by a small collection of nineteenth-century Chinese bowls in the Victoria & Albert Museum, London. The bowls display carefully arranged groups of bamboo stems and leaves with blossoms, shown in white on the rich background of Chinese red colouring.

The evening purse shows a single bamboo motif worked in Satin Stitch on glazed or satinized cotton which has been lightly quilted to add interest and richness to the plain fabric.

To complement the purse, I decorated the corners of three white cotton lawn handkerchiefs with a smaller version of the bamboo motif, each one being worked in a slightly different shade of the rusty Chinese red colour.

MATERIALS

3 white cotton lawn handkerchiefs with simple hemstitch edging

Coats Anchor stranded embroidery cotton: small amounts of Light Rust 337, Mid Rust 339, Dark Rust 20

Chinese red satinized or glazed cotton furnishing fabric, 40 × 115cm (16 × 45in)

White cotton backing fabric, 40 × 56 cm (16 × 22 in) and 30 × 45 cm (12 × 18 in)

White silky fabric, 30 × 45 cm (12 × 18 in)

Coats Coton Perlé No. 5 thread, 2 skeins Dark Rust 340; 1 skein White 1

Sewing thread to match satinized or glazed cotton

Basting thread

A little double knitting wool, any colour

Medium-weight polyester or terylene wadding, 40 × 56 cm (16 × 22 in)

Tracing paper

Fabric transfer pencil, blue or other colour to show up on the fabric

Brown- or red-coloured crayon

Wooden hoop, 10 cm (4 in) diameter

Rectangular embroidery frame, 36 × 50 cm (14 × 20 in)

Stitches used: *Satin Stitch, Back Stitch, Basting Stitch, machine Straight Stitch, Slip Stitch.*

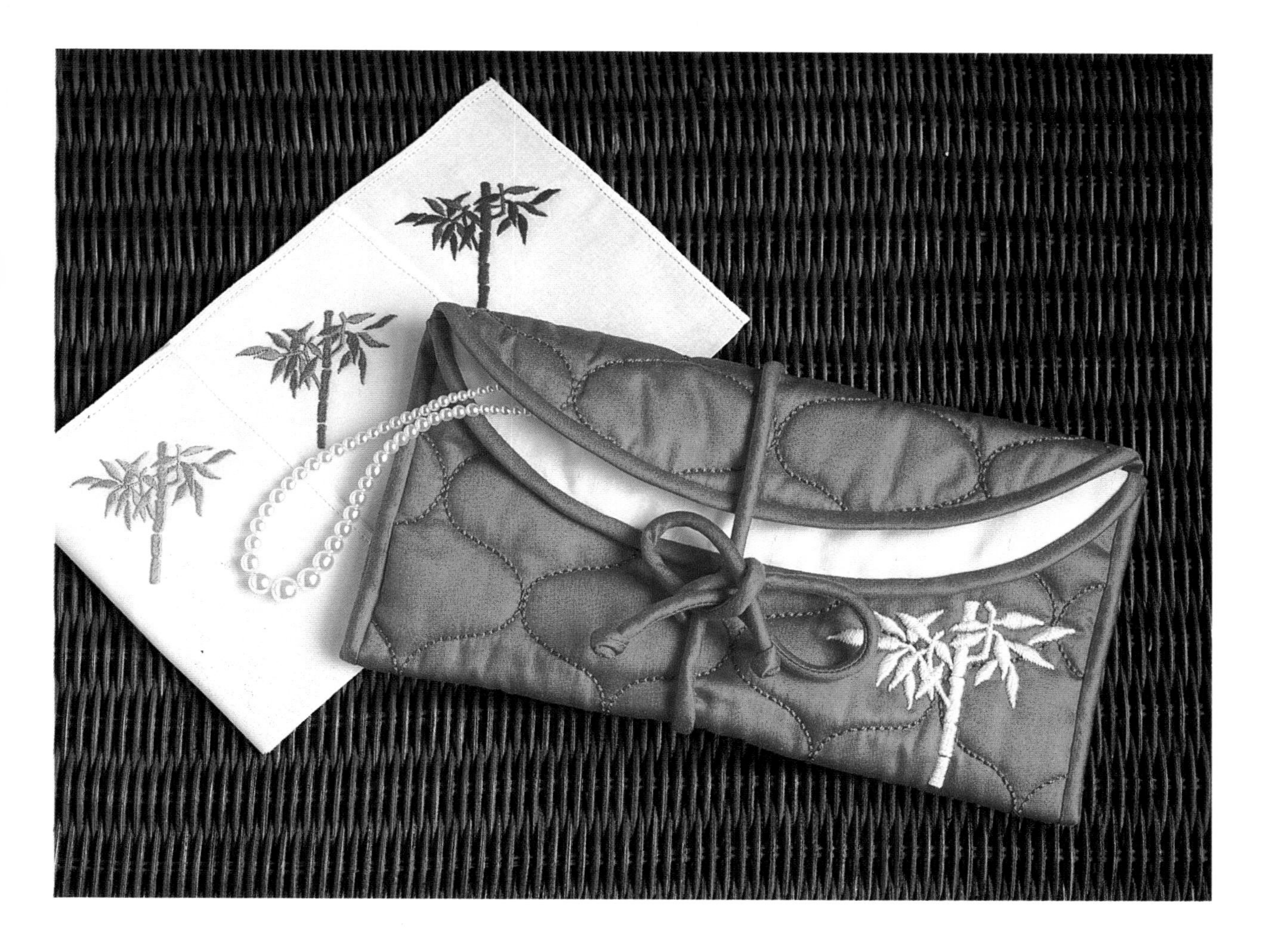

The bolder white motif of the purse has been achieved by using Coton Perlé thread while the stranded thread was used on the handkerchiefs to give a finer effect.

TO EMBROIDER THE HANDKERCHIEFS

1 Press the handkerchiefs to remove any creases. Position one corner of each handkerchief (in turn) over the small trace-off motif of the bamboo design (opposite). Check that you can place the area to be embroidered within the small hoop. Using the coloured crayon with a very sharp point accurately trace the design on to the fabric with clear but fine marks. Remember all these marks must be covered with stitchery if the end results is to look neat and effective.

2 Stretch each handkerchief in turn within the small hoop and using one shade of stranded thread per handkerchief, work the design entirely in Satin Stitch. Use two strands of thread and work the stitches straight across the bamboo stems and slant them across the pointed leaves.

3 When you have completed each handkerchief press it gently on the wrong side with a steam iron to remove any creases and also to encourage an embossed effect of the stitchery.

TO MAKE THE EVENING PURSE

1 Stretch the larger piece of white cotton backing fabric over the rectangular frame and lay the terylene or polyester wadding over it.

Press the Chinese red fabric to remove any creases and lay it out on a clean, flat surface. Following the cutting plan on page 51, cut out a rectangle measuring 40×56 cm (16×22 in)

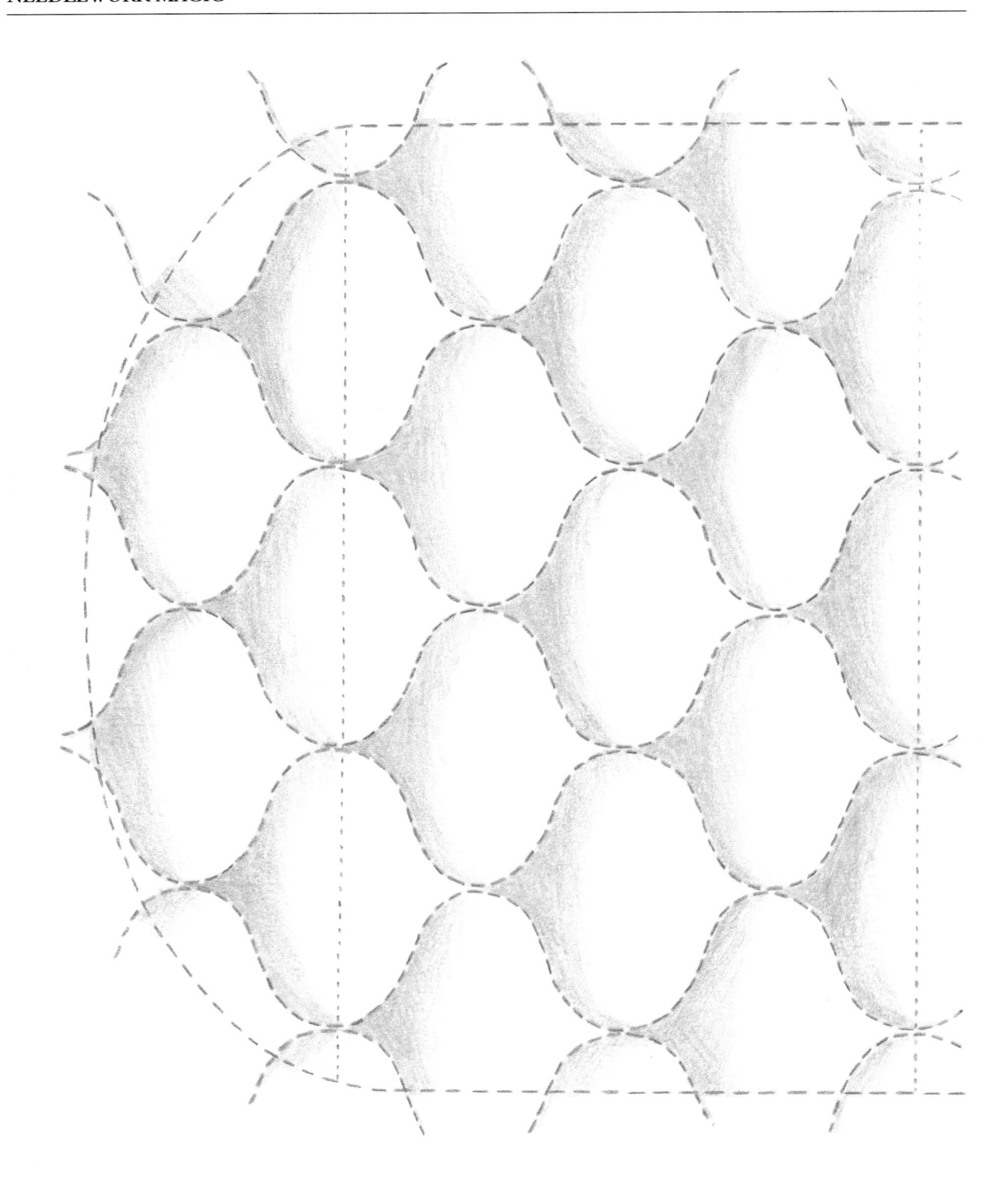

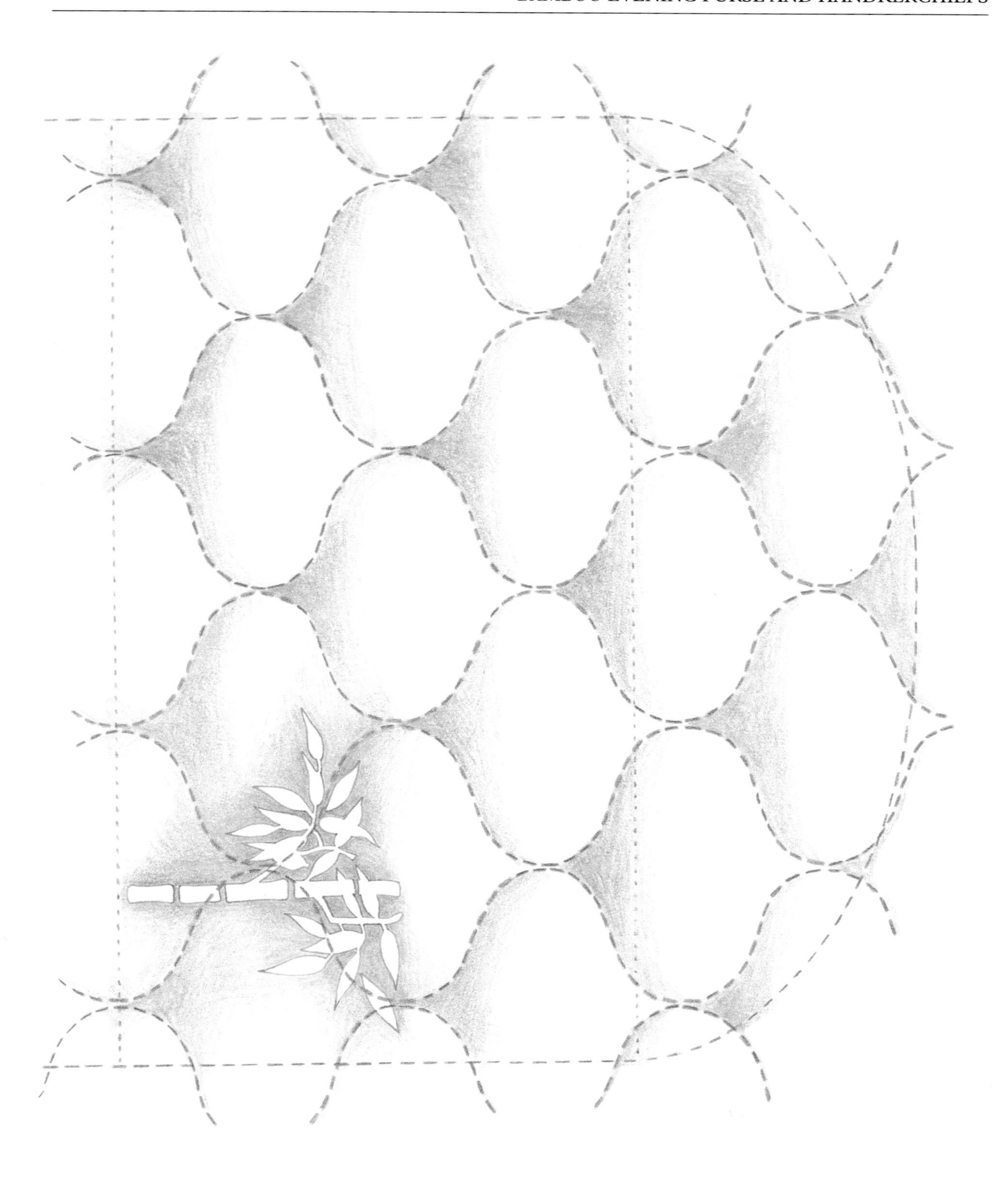

The outer dotted line is the seam line; the inner lines are fold lines. The design is shown here in two halves and a small central strip has been repeated on both sides. When you make your trace-off pattern you need to have only one centre fold line so align the two halves accordingly.

from one end; then cut out three bias strips from the remaining piece. To find the true bias of the fabric simply fold the bottom left-hand corner up to the top edge so that the left-hand edge matches the top edge. The bias of the fabric will be along the fold line. Press this and use as a guide to cut out the three parallel strips.

Reserve the three strips to be used for binding around the purse and making the cord (step 9).

2 Place the rectangle of Chinese red fabric over the frame on top of the wadding. Smooth the layers together and attach the fabric to the sides of the frame without pulling it to much as this would flatten the wadding beneath it. You are aiming for a smooth, soft effect rather than a very taut one.

3 Prepare your transfer pattern using the trace-off pattern on pages 48–9. Using a photocopier, enlarge the design from A4 to A3 size. (When enlarged it will measure 24.5 × 40.5 cm (9½ × 16 in) from seam line to seam line.) Trace this on to a sheet of good-quality tracing paper using a fine-tipped felt pen. On the wrong side of the tracing paper carefully and accurately trace with the transfer pencil the quilting pattern and the bamboo motif; do not trace the dotted guidelines which are referred to later on when making up the purse.

NB: Following the manufacturer's instructions, carry out a small test to see how strong the transfer marks are. You may need to press more or less firmly on the paper. Remember you need only a light mark that is just visible enough to see and embroider over.

Using an iron as directed, transfer the design on to the prepared fabric centring the design within the frame and taking care not to allow the tracing paper to move whilst ironing. A few carefully placed dressmaker's pins at the corners of the paper will help but take care not to catch them with the plate of the iron.

Reserve the tracing-paper pattern.

4 You are now ready to commence stitching. Work the bamboo motif in Satin Stitch, using the White Coton Perlé thread. Work this in the same way as those on the handkerchiefs (see step 2 page 47).

5 When the motif is complete work the quilting pattern entirely in Back Stitch using the Dark Rust Coton Perlé thread. Work from the bamboo motif outwards and take extra care to keep your stitches neat and even in size in order to achieve a regular effect.

6 When the quilting is complete cut out the tracing paper pattern along the outer dotted seam line. Pin the pattern over the quilted fabric carefully aligning the bamboo motif and the quilting design. Baste accurately around the pattern. Then fold the pattern along one of the fold lines and baste along its edge to mark the fold line on the fabric. Re-fold the pattern along each of the other two fold lines and baste along each one.

7 Release the fabric layers from the frame and trim away the surplus fabric leaving a 1 cm (⅜ in) allowance around the outer seam line.

8 Press the remaining piece of white cotton fabric and the silky fabric to remove any creases and place them on the wrong side of the quilted shape with the right side of the silky fabric facing uppermost.

Pin and baste all the layers together. Trim away the excess fabric to match the quilted shape.

9 Join two of the bias lengths together to give a long strip ready to make into binding strips. With the use of a steam iron fold the strip in half lengthwise with wrong sides facing and press the fold lightly. Open the pressed strip and fold the edges in so that they meet at the centre and press to hold in shape. (You can purchase quite cheaply, from most good haberdashery departments, a very effective tool specifically deigned to make bias binding strips.)

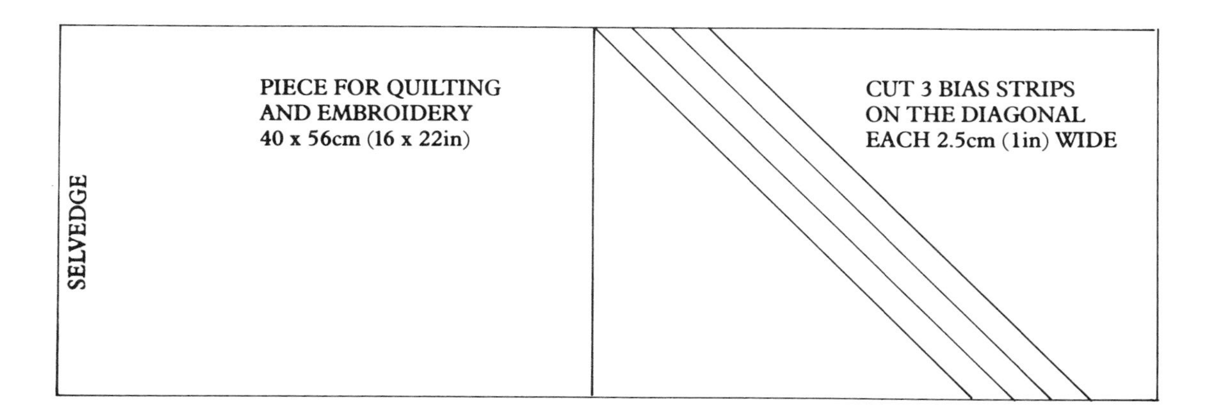

The cutting plan for the Chinese red cotton fabric.

With right sides together fold the third strip in half lengthwise, pin and baste to hold. With matching sewing thread and your sewing machine set to Straight Stitch, work along the length of this strip taking a narrow 6 mm (¼ in) seam allowance. Remove the basting stitches and, with the aid of a small safety pin, turn the strip to the right side (see Lucky Bats step 9 page 98). Trim the ends of the strip.

With a large-eyed needle thread several lengths of the knitting wool through the bias strip to give a softly filled cord. Trim the woollen strands so that they are slightly shorter than the fabric tube by gently pulling the wool so that it stretches, cut it and then let it go and you will find that it shrinks inside the fabric tube neatly.

Tuck the raw ends of the tube inside itself and with matching thread hand-sew the folded edges together. Neatly tie a knot at each end of the fabric cord to give it a finished look.

10 Make up the purse.

Attach the long bias-binding strip carefully around the entire shape of the purse working with the right side of the bias binding and the quilted side of the purse facing each other. To achieve a neat look, aim to have the two joins in the bias strip at the back of the purse.

NB: You have a 1 cm (⅜ in) allowance round the seam line of your purse shape but your binding allowance from raw edge to first fold is smaller so make sure you match this fold line with the basted seam line.

Pin, baste and then machine Straight Stitch the binding in position around the purse shape folding in one of the raw ends of the binding to neaten the point of starting and finishing. If you do this diagonally you will achieve a very neat join.

Trim away the excess fabric close to the line of stitching.

11 Turn the bias binding around the raw edge of the purse shape. Pin the folded bias binding to the white silky side of the purse. With matching thread, hand Slip Stitch the binding to the line of machine stitching to hold.

12 Fold the purse in half along the centre basted guideline and pin to hold. With a double length of matching thread carefully and securely stitch the bound edges of the purse together on each side working from the fold up to the line of basting on the front of the purse. Make sure you work tiny stitches that will not show yet make them strong enough to hold the sides of the purse together effectively. Work a few stitches back towards the lower edge of the purse before securely finishing off the thread.

Remove the guideline basting stitches.

13 Finally, tie your fabric cord around the purse and choose where to attach it to the purse. You may decide to attach it to the upper flap, or to the lower edge of the purse, or to leave it unattached.

Butterflies and Blossom Picture

This delightful miniature picture could just as easily be made into a greetings card for a very special occasion. As a picture, it will enhance any wall with its jewelled detail and rich texture and colouring. If you prefer to make the butterfly picture into a greetings card, simply make your own presentation card of the required size (see page 139) and mount the stretched embroidery within it.

My original watercolour study from which the design progressed. This was inspired by a finely embroidered Chinese sleeveband. Even at this early stage I was conscious of the stitch direction and the amount of detail required.

MATERIALS

Apple-green glazed cotton, 35 × 40 cm (14 × 16 in)
White cotton backing fabric, 35 × 40 cm (14 × 16 in)
Pelmet or heavyweight interfacing (Vilene), 14 × 21 cm (5½ × 8¼ in)
Coats Anchor stranded embroidery thread: 2 skeins each Blue 118, 119, 120; 1 skein each Mauve 85, 94, Brown 352, Green 189, White 1, Gold 306, Cream 778
Buttonhole thread to lace the embroidery over the cardboard
Basting thread
Rigid cardboard to stretch embroidery over, 18.5 × 24 cm (7¼ × 9½ in)
Double-sided sticky tape
Rectangular embroidery frame, 30 × 35 cm (12 × 14 in)
Good quality tracing paper
Black fine-tipped felt pen
Blue-coloured crayon

Stitches used: *Basting Stitch, Satin Stitch, French Knots, Back Stitch, Straight Stitch, Encroaching Straight Stitch.*

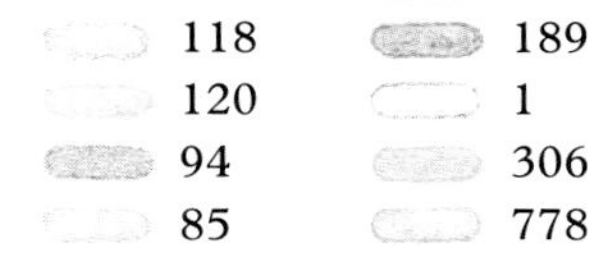
119
118
120
94
85
352
189
1
306
778

TO MAKE THE BUTTERFLIES AND BLOSSOM PICTURE

1 Using the tracing paper and the felt pen, make two tracings of the butterfly design and its floral border pattern. Trace all the detail carefully and accurately on to one sheet of tracing paper, but on the second one you do not need to trace the fine detail of the stamens of the flowers, and the antennae and legs of the butterflies.

Reserve the complete tracing.

2 Use the second simplified tracing to cut out all the design shapes accurately from the interfacing as follows. Cut strips of the double-sided sticky tape and use them to attach the simplified design securely to the interfacing. Then with a pair of sharp-pointed trimming scissors cut out all the main shapes of the butterfly design. If you look at the photograph (opposite) you will see that the areas of solid stitchery have a raised and embossed effect. This has been achieved by embroidering over the interfacing shapes, so cut out all the shapes accurately. If one design area is adjoining another (for example, the two wings of the top right butterfly), then cut them out as one shape. To help you organize this process and prevent all the tiny shapes getting muddled as you cut them out, place them in their correct position on the original trace-off pattern (see page 53). You do not need to use the tracing to cut out all the individual petals of the blossom on the border pattern, you can simply cut out lots of tiny circles and some half circles using the tracing to guide you.

3 Prepare your fabric as follows:

Press the green fabric on the wrong side to remove any creases.

Press and then stretch the white backing fabric on to the frame, ensuring the grain of the fabric is parallel with the sides of the frame. Stretch the green fabric (shiny side uppermost) over the frame on top of the backing fabric.

4 Place the detailed tracing of the design centrally on top of the stretched fabric aligning the straight edges of the design with the sides of the frame. With basting thread stitch the tracing paper temporarily in position around the outer edges of the design.

Carefully insert a pair of sharp-pointed paper scissors into the traced design at one corner of the central butterfly design and with great care cut around three sides of the design, leaving it attached along the fourth side. This will enable you to lift up the tracing paper when positioning your interfacing shapes.

5 Carefully and accurately place the cut interfacing shapes in position on the green fabric using the traced design to guide you. Remember to peel off the pieces of tracing paper that are attached to the interfacing shapes before positioning them on the green fabric. Baste each shape in place as you work across the design.

6 When you have attached all the cut shapes to the green background then you can cut along the fourth side of the paper design to detach the butterfly section but leave the border design attached to the stretched fabric

Use the crayon (make sure it has a very sharp point) to draw in the detail of the pattern of each butterfly wing on to the interfacing shapes.

Trim away the tracing paper along the inner edge of the border design. Snip the tracing paper from the inner corners of the border to the outer points so that each side of the border can be folded back to reveal the fabric underneath. Then using the traced design in the same way as before, align the tiny interfacing petals and baste them in place. Do not draw the crazed pattern on to the fabric.

7 You are now ready to start stitching. Use two strands of embroidery thread at all times unless otherwise indicated.

It does not really matter where you start but you will probably find it better to work some of the smaller, simpler

shapes to begin with while you are familiarizing yourself with the design and its techniques. Refer to the photograph on page 55 to see in which direction to work the areas of Satin Stitch. Most of the shapes are covered with evenly-worked Satin Stitch which is built up across the width rather than the length of a shape, as this allows shorter stitches which can be more effectively controlled. When working the wings, the Satin Stitches are always worked so that they appear to be growing outwards from the base of each wing towards the fluted edge. Where an area is rather large causing the stitches to be very long or if you need to create a curved effect then turn your Satin Stitches into Encroaching Satin Stitches which are ideal for such areas (see page 82). Similarly when working the narrow bands of white feathery markings on the butterfly wings, work the white Satin Stitches so that they encroach into the next area of stitchery. Keep referring to the photograph of the finished embroidery and also the trace-off pattern, to guide you while you stitch and to help you to select the correct colours. Work tiny clusters of French Knots and single French Knots to add the 'eyes' to the butterfly wings and work lines of minute Back Stitches on top of the Satin Stitches in the appropriate positions.

Work the legs and antennae of the butterflies in tiny Back Stitches. Try to work them 'freehand' without drawing on the fabric as the stitching is too fine to cover any crayon marks. Remember you can always remove a misplaced stitch whereas the crayon mark is more permanent and unsightly.

The eyes are worked as mid-Blue and Brown French Knots.

The abstract filling shapes and the blossoms are worked in the three shades of Blue. The blossoms are worked in pale Blue and then have a few highlighting mid-Blue stitches added with the central circles of dark Blue. Each flower is then finished with White Straight Stitches and French Knots to represent the stamens.

Work all the outer edges of this part of the design as straight as possible to create an invisible border line around the design.

8 Next work the border design of the flowers and the abstract 'crazed' pattern.

The blossom petals are worked individually in Satin Stitches with Single Straight Stitches representing the stamens.

Work the crazed pattern using your tracing as a guide (this is still attached to the fabric). Work the slightly thicker lines in Back Stitches (these are shown on the trace-off pattern). Then, using a single strand of thread, work the fine detail of the pattern quite freely in Straight Stitches to build up the crazed effect.

9 When you have completed the embroidery remove all the basting threads and also the tracing paper. Then carefully remove the fabric from the frame (see page 133).

Place the cardboard centrally over the wrong side of the embroidery and cut away the surplus fabric leaving enough to turn over to the wrong side of the cardboard and lace in position (4–5 cm (1½ in–2 in) will be sufficient). Using a long, double length of buttonhole thread carefully lace the embroidery in position on the cardboard (see page 140). Frequently check the position of the embroidery to ensure you achieve a smooth and even effect.

Your miniature picture is now complete and you can choose whether to make it into a very special greetings card or have it framed to make a wall picture. Do not place it behind glass or you will lose the richly embossed effect of the raised stitches.

Flowers and Fans Cushion

This boldly-coloured cushion is worked entirely in Tent Stitch. The strength of the design is such that there is no need nor indeed room to add a variety of textures by using different stitches. The rich areas of blue and terracotta confidently form the main shapes and are complemented by small areas of jade-green and sandy-gold to give a full and lively design.

The cushion has three design areas: a central section of simple, bold flower shapes; a narrow inner border of a randomly worked 'broken' pattern; an outer border of richly-coloured fan shapes.

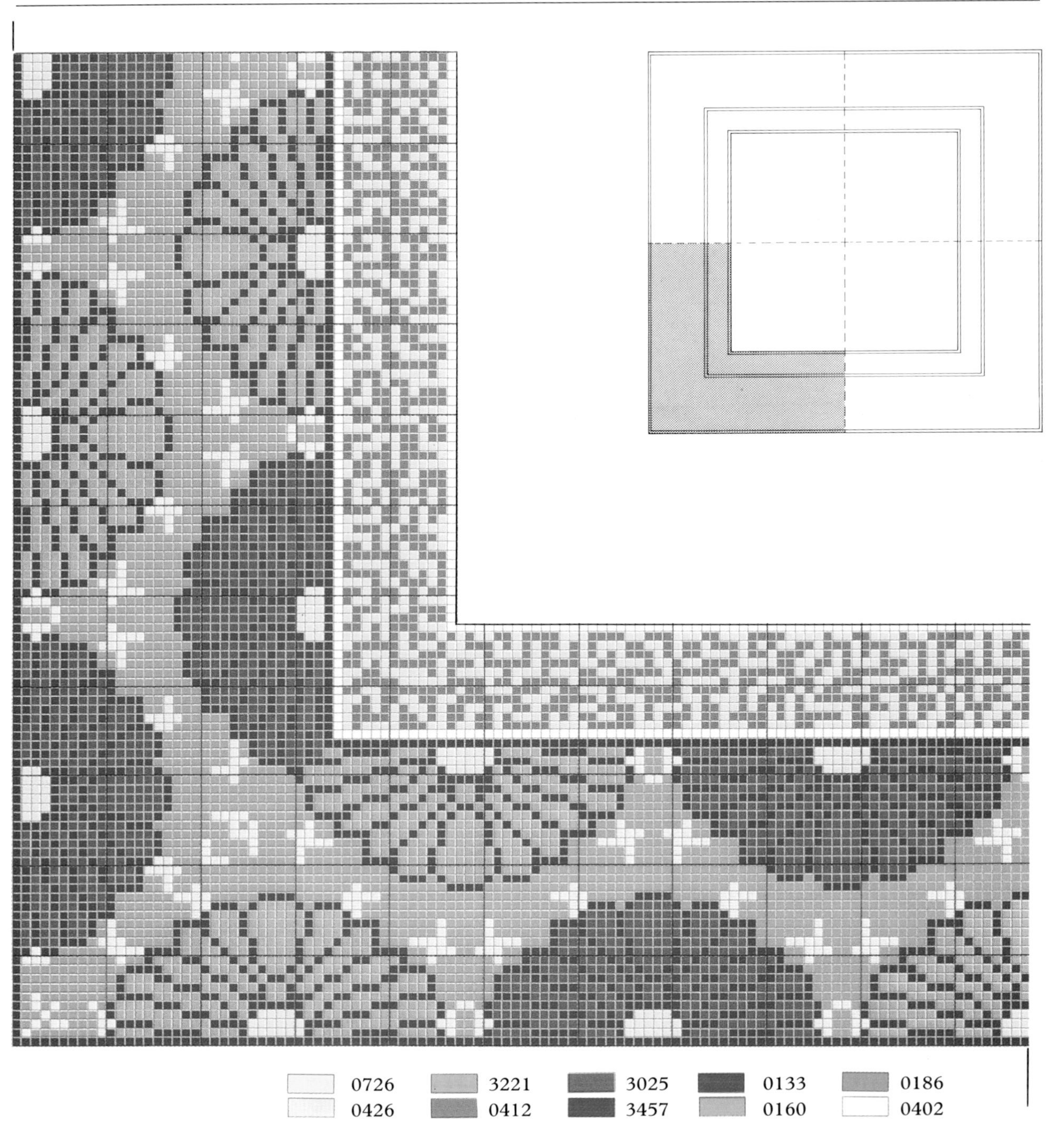

This chart shows one quarter of the border section which surrounds the centre flowers image (see overleaf). Repeat this section four times, turning your frame 90° for each quarter.

MATERIALS

White mono canvas (15 holes per in), 56 cm (22 in) square
Coats tapisserie wool: 6 skeins Blue 0133; 5 skeins each Blue 0160, Terracotta 3025, 3221; 4 skeins each Terracotta 0412, White 0402; 3 skeins Terracotta 0426; 2 skeins each Blue 3457, Sand 0726; 1 skein Jade 0186
Blue fabric to back cushion, 43 cm (17 in) square
Cushion pad, 40 cm (16 in) square
Sewing thread to match backing fabric
Wooden frame, 50 cm (20 in) square
Waterproof marking pen to mark canvas

Stitches used: *Tent Stitch, machine Straight Stitch, Slip Stitch.*

TO MAKE THE CUSHION

1 Stretch the canvas on the frame, ensuring the threads are parallel to the sides of the frame.

2 Find the centre of the canvas by counting the threads and then lightly mark the horizontal and vertical centre guidelines to establish the centre of the canvas (the centre point is a hole and not an intersection of threads).

Each square of the chart represents one Tent Stitch, which is worked over one horizontal and one vertical thread of canvas.

It does not really matter where you start your stitchery. You can start in the centre or you may find it beneficial to count along one of the guidelines and begin your stitching with the blue and white lines which lie on each side of the randomly patterned inner border.

Wherever you choose to begin remember to work each colour as economically as possible, beginning and finishing off a yarn securely and not jumping across the wrong side of the canvas from one area to another – finish off and then start again instead. Do not use very long lengths of yarn as the action of passing the soft woollen yarn backwards and forwards through the holes of the tough canvas will gradually wear it thin. Never attempt to work a stitch in one single move. This will strain the canvas and distort the stitchery as an uneven tension is likely to be the result. (Working within a frame discourages this lazy way of stitching and encourages a good even tension.)

3 Follow the chart accurately and gradually build up the design. Frequently check that you have not made

any errors as it is easy to count one square too many or too few. If you make a mistake it is easy, with a little patience, to unpick and remove the stitches and re-work them correctly.

4 When you work the random pattern of the inner border use the chart to show you the way the pattern has been built up but you do not need to copy it stitch for stitch. You will soon feel confident to make it up as you move around the narrow border band.

When you reach the outer border you will find it easier to work the fans around the inner edge, then count outwards and establish the outer edge of the cushion before working the outer fans. Then fill in the background areas.

5 Once you have completed the entire design remove the canvas from the frame and trim away the excess leaving a 1 cm (3/8 in) seam allowance on all sides. With right sides facing, pin, then baste and machine Straight Stitch the cushion face and back together along the edge of the canvaswork stitchery. Remember to leave an opening along one side to push the cushion pad in.

Carefully clip across the seam allowance at the corners. Turn to the right side and fill with the cushion pad. Fold in the seam allowance along the opening and Slip Stitch the folded edges together to close.

This is the centre section of the cushion showing the flowers design. It is surrounded by the border (see the chart on page 58).

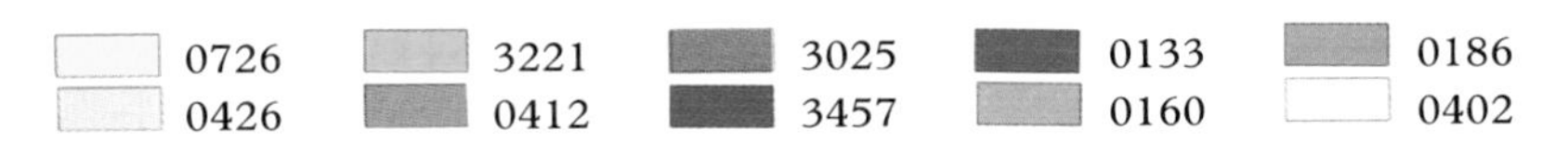

Blue and Yellow Floral Table Mats

These boldly coloured cross-stitch mats will create a striking table for any dinner party. I made them in Cross Stitch using only three shades of blue to give a simple yet very effective result worked on the ever-popular Aida fabric. I dyed some white Aida fabric as I wanted a strong sunshine yellow colour. (If you do not want to dye your fabric then buy yellow fabric instead or, if you prefer, work the blue design on white fabric, which will be very pleasing to the eye.)

This design is ideal for experimentation. Just because it has been created for Cross Stitch does not mean you have to work it in this way. Why not interpret it into canvaswork? Use Tent Stitch on mono canvas, working the background as well as the floral design in the original colours or try your own colour scheme. Make a small sample piece to ensure that you like the effect before starting to work a place setting.

The finished diameter of each place mat is 32 cm (12¾ in) and that of the drinks mat is 14 cm (5½ in). Both incorporate a layer of insulating fabric to protect your table from heat.

MATERIALS

(for a single setting of one place mat and matching drinks mat)

Aida 14 count fabric, white or sunshine yellow, 50 × 75 cm (20 × 30 in)
Blue backing fabric, 38 × 60 cm (15 × 24 in)
Table insulating fabric, 38 × 60 cm (15 × 24 in)
Coats Anchor stranded embroidery thread: 2 skeins each Blue 127, 132, 145
Royal blue silky cord, 160 cm (1¾ yd) long
Sewing thread to match cord
Basting thread
Dylon Hand Dye colour 01 Yellow permanent colouring for natural fabrics (only if dyeing white fabric)
Tracing paper, a large sheet
Rectangular frame, 43 cm (17 in) square
Wooden embroidery hoop, 17 cm (7 in) diameter
A pair of compasses

Stitches used: *Cross Stitch, machine Straight Stitch, Slip Stitch.*

NB: Decide how many place settings you want to make and calculate how much fabric you will need in total. The amount given above is a generous measurement, enough for you to work one place mat and two drinks mats if divided carefully into one large piece 50 cm (20 in) square and two small pieces each measuring 25 cm (10 in) square. As Aida fabric is quite expensive I suggest you work out carefully exactly how much you will need.

If you are going to dye your fabric do this in one lot in order to achieve an even colouring and follow the dye manufacturer's instructions carefully.

TO WORK THE LARGE DESIGN

1 Having divided your evenweave fabric as directed (see above) stretch the larger piece over the rectangular frame ensuring the grain of the fabric lies straight and the threads are parallel with the sides of the frame.

2 Find and mark with Basting Stitches the horizontal and vertical centre guidelines to give the centre of the fabric (this will be a hole in the fabric).

3 Carefully count outwards along one of the guidelines to the point where you wish to begin stitching. (You can,

if you wish, start at the centre point and then work outwards, but it is advisable to start with a clearly recognisable and easily counted shape to work until you become familiar with the design.)

4 Use two strands of thread at all times. All the upper stitches of the Cross Stitches must face the same direction to achieve a smooth and effective result.

5 Work the central design and then count outwards along the horizontal guideline to the border design and work this. Work one of the quarter sections shown overleaf and then repeat it three more times around the central motif. You will find the entwining border pattern joins and becomes a continuous design as you work each quarter section.

6 Once your design is complete remove the fabric from the frame. Gently press the wrong side of the

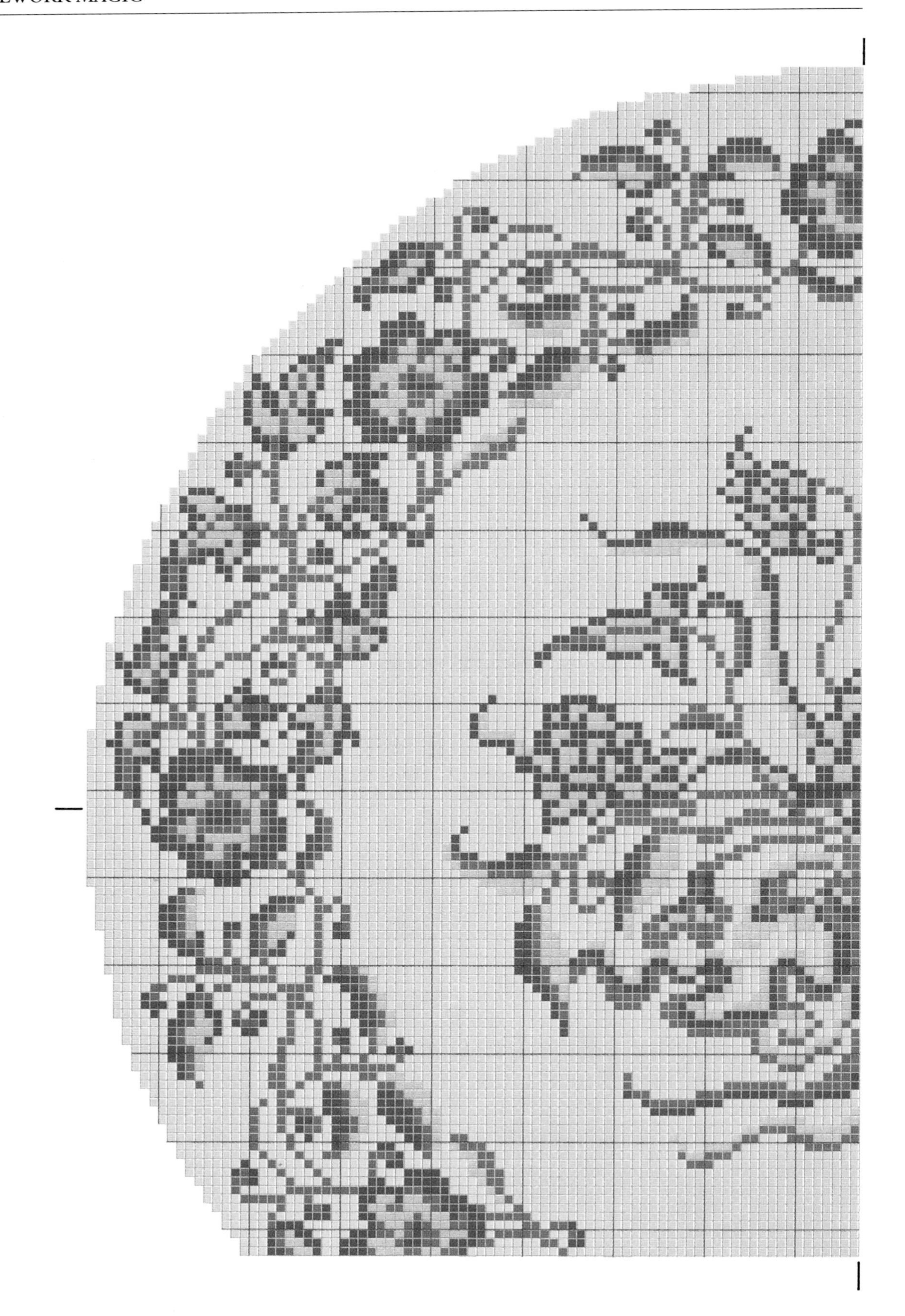

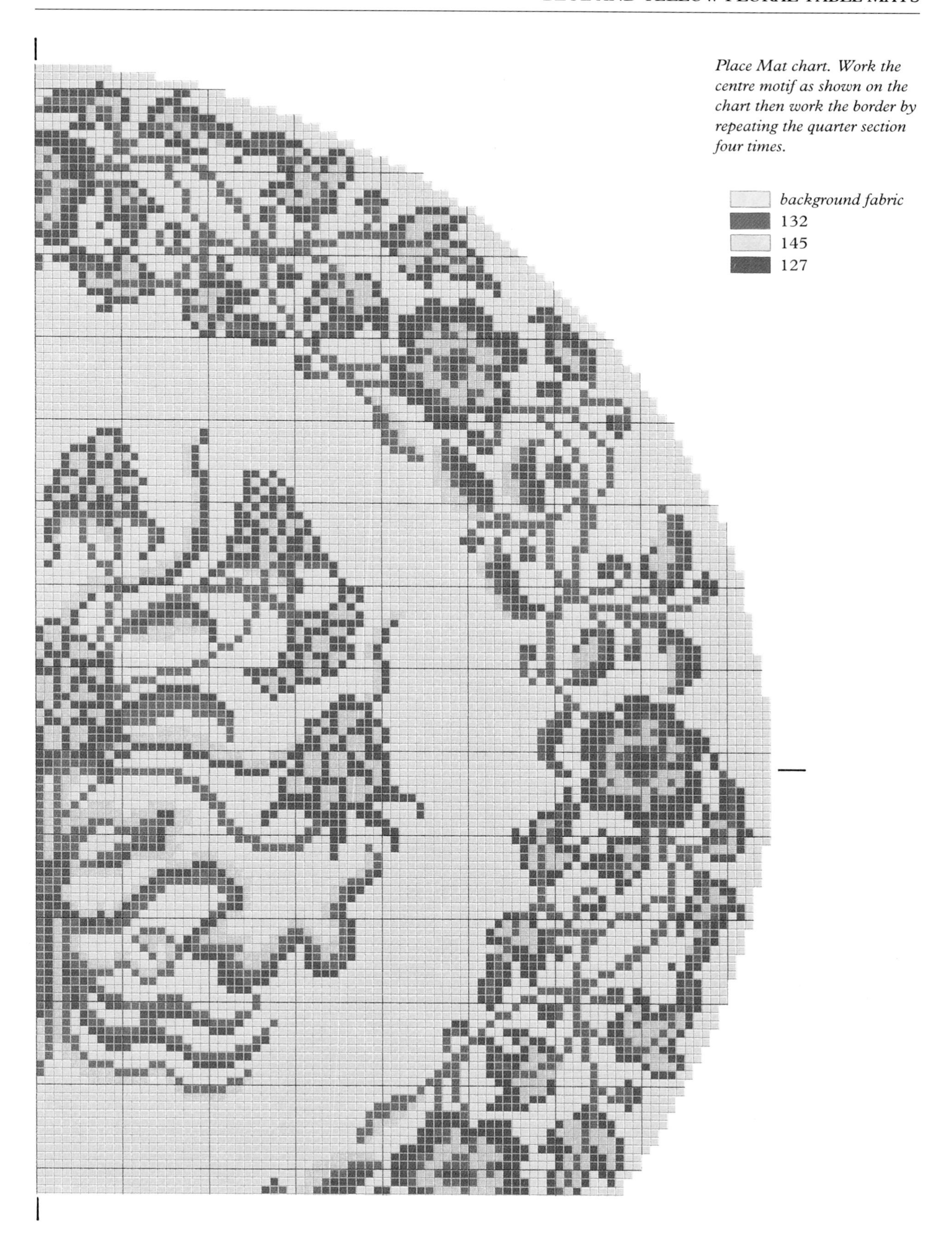

Place Mat chart. Work the centre motif as shown on the chart then work the border by repeating the quarter section four times.

fabric with a steam iron to encourage an embossed effect.
7 Using the pair of compasses draw a large circle 32 cm (12½ in) diameter at one end of the large sheet of tracing paper, draw a smaller circle 14 cm (5½ in) diameter at the other end of the paper and cut out each circle accurately. Reserve the smaller circle to be used as a template when making up the drinks mat.
8 Align the centre point (pierced by the compasses) of the large template with the centre of the wrong side of your embroidery (use your guidelines to help you). Carefully pin the paper template to the fabric without moving it.

Trim away the excess yellow (or white) fabric leaving a 1 cm (⅜ in) seam allowance all around the template.

Press the blue backing fabric on the wrong side to remove any creases. Then place the yellow circle of embroidered fabric over one end of the blue fabric (with right sides together) and pin the layers together, keeping the paper template in position. Trim away the excess blue fabric reserving the excess to be used to back the drinks mat.

Baste around the edge of the template through both layers of fabric. Remove and reserve the template then, with blue sewing thread, machine Straight Stitch along the seam line. Leave an opening large enough to slip the insulating fabric in later (step 10).

Snip the seam allowance around the curved seam line to encourage a smooth shape when turned to the right side.

Carefully turn to the right side, ease into shape and press gently on the backing side.
9 Using the tracing-paper template cut out a circle of insulating fabric. Then trim it all around to make it slightly smaller than the embroidered place mat. (Trim away no more than 3 mm (⅛ in) to start with then, if necessary, you can remove a little more depending on the thickness of your insulating fabric.)
10 Ease the insulating circle into position inside the embroidered mat. Tuck in the open edges of the mat and hand Slip Stitch the folded edges of the opening together, leaving a tiny gap just big enough to tuck the raw ends of the blue cord into.
11 With matching thread hand-stitch the blue cord around the edges of the mat, neatly hiding the cut ends of the cord in the gap left in the seam line. Stitch the gap closed to complete the place mat.

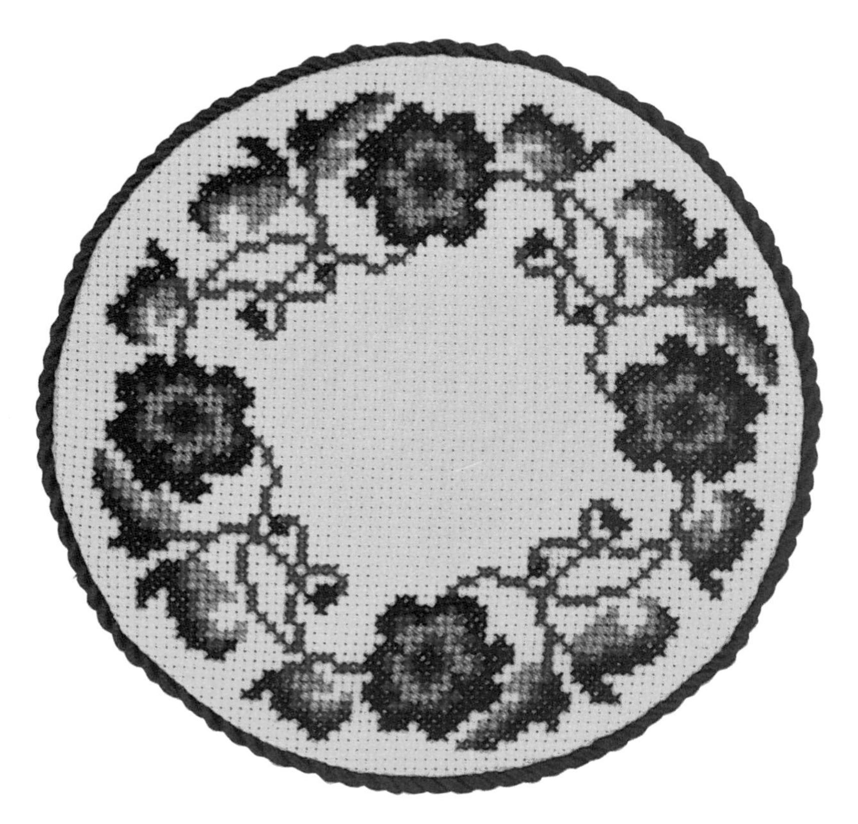

To work this Drinks Mat (left) follow the chart and instructions opposite.

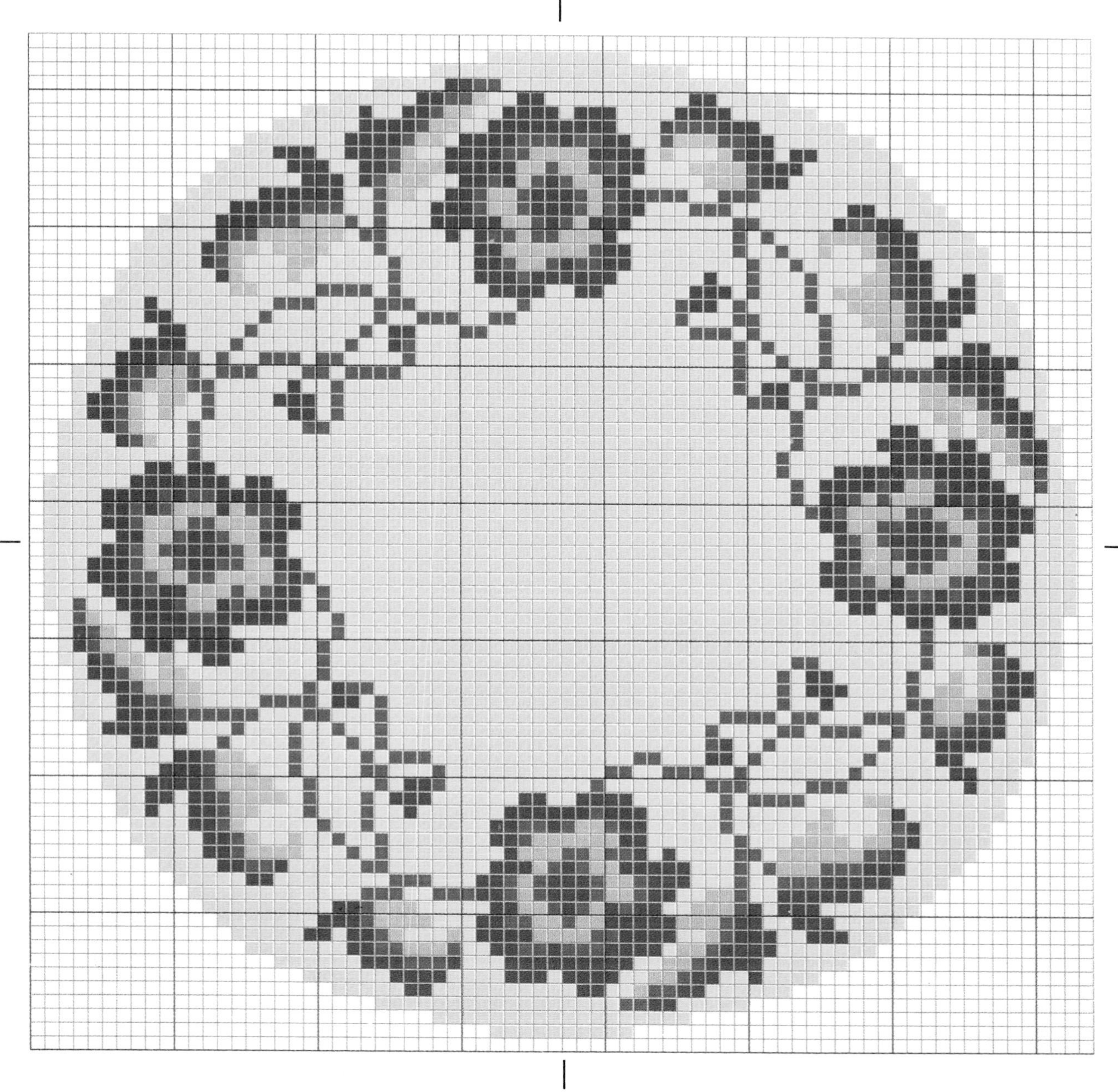

TO MAKE THE DRINKS MAT

1 Stretch the smaller piece of yellow fabric within the hoop, ensuring the grain is straight.

2 Find the centre of the working area and mark with Basting Stitches as for the large mat.

3 Count outwards from the centre along one of the guidelines to find a suitable starting point.

Repeat the quarter section of the border design (see chart above) four times to give a circular border pattern.

4 Make up the drinks mat in the same way as the place mat, using the small paper template (follow steps 6–11 opposite.)

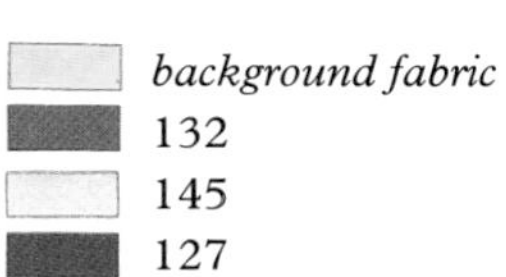

Riverside Ducks Cushion

This boldly patterned cushion was inspired by a delightfully naïve design of ducks and water plants that I found on a child's kimono in the Victoria & Albert Museum, London.

The decorative pattern on the kimono was made by resist stencilling, a method which is particularly effective for relatively simple and bold shapes. First, you treat all the areas of fabric you do not want to be coloured with dyes with a resisting paste (a substance that prevents the fabric from absorbing dyes). Then you colour the remaining areas of the fabric either by submerging it in a dye bath or painting with a brush.

When designing and making this cushion I decided to echo the character of the original printed design using fabric transfer dye crayons. These are wax crayons that contain dyes and are quick and simple to use. You draw the design on to paper and then iron this against fabric. The heat of the iron not only transfers the design by melting the wax crayoning but also fixes the dye on the fabric. It is a fast and extremely effective method of printing fabric when only a small one-off area of printing is required.

MATERIALS

Cream linen-type fabric with a rough weave, two pieces – 56 cm (22 in) square, 42 cm (16½ in) square
White cotton backing fabric, 56 cm (22 in) square
Grey velvet ribbon, 1 cm (⅜ in) wide and 1.4 m (1½ yd) long
Grey velvet ribbon, 1.5 cm (⅝ in) wide and 1.85 m (2 yd) long
No. 2 piping cord, 1.85 m (2 yd)
Grey sewing thread to match velvet ribbon
Basting thread
Crayola fabric transfer dye crayons
Coats Soft Embroidery cotton thread, approximately 1 skein each: Rust 339, 337, Brown 349, 365, 888, Grey 815, 8581, Blue 838, 850, Green 217, 266, 216, 213
Fine-tipped black felt pen
Cushion pad, 40 cm (16 in) square
Tracing paper, 3 sheets A3 size
Layout paper, 1 sheet A3 size
Wooden frame, 50 cm (20 in)

Stitches used: *Back Stitch, French Knots, Running Stitch, Seeding Stitch, machine Straight Stitch.*

888
365
349
337
339
850
213
266
216
217
8581
815
838

TO MAKE THE CUSHION:

1 Using the sheet of layout paper enlarge the central square section of the design on page 69, doubling it in size so that it measures 28 cm (11 in) square. You can do this by drawing a square of this size and dividing it up equally into sixteen smaller squares, each measuring 7 cm (2¾ in). Then transfer the design on to this grid, enlarging it with the aid of the grid lines (see Special Techniques, page 133). Alternatively, if you have access to a photocopier that can enlarge and reduce material then you can easily and quickly enlarge the design to the correct size.

Once you have enlarged the design trace it accurately, using the felt pen, on to one of the sheets of tracing paper.

2 Trace the corner section of the border pattern on to one half of a second sheet of tracing paper, positioning it so that you can then draw a second corner section next to it to form one half of the border. Then trace this on to the remaining sheet of tracing paper to produce the second half of the border.

3 Following the manufacturer's instructions (also see Special Techniques, page 135) make a test strip of the different colours which can be achieved with the dye crayons. (Make your test strip along one edge of the larger square of linen-type fabric.) Remember you can blend them and vary their strength of colour.

Use the crayons to colour in the underside of the tracing paper with the two half border sections and the inner square. Refer closely to the finished cushion (see page 68) to help you choose your colours. Looking at the colours of the Soft Embroidery threads will also help you. The overall colouring is one of muted natural shades of greys, browns, greens, blues and rusts.

888
365
349
337
339
850
213
266
216
217
8581
815
838

centre

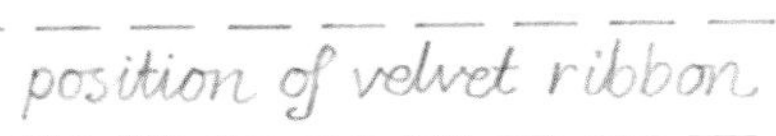

4 Press the larger piece of cream linen-type fabric to remove any creases. Once more following the manufacturer's instructions carefully transfer the square design on to the centre of the fabric aligning the sides of the design with the straight grain of the fabric. Remember to place the transfer waxy side down on the fabric and take great care not to move the transfer paper when you use the iron as any movement will create a blurred image.

Place one half of the border transfer in position, aligning the broken guide-lines of the border around the central square. Double-check it is correctly placed before applying the iron to it.

Repeat this process with the second half of the border.

Keep the three pieces of tracing paper – you will need them when finishing the cushion.

5 Stretch the white cotton backing fabric and then the linen-type fabric on the wooden frame, making sure the crayonned design is centrally positioned and that the straight grain of the fabric is parallel to the sides of the frame.

6 You are now ready to work the embroidery. Use neat and even Back Stitches to outline all the design shapes allowing the colour changes of the crayonning to influence your choice of thread colour. If you refer to the photograph on page 68 you will see that two or even three colours have been used on a single leaf, flower or duck. (Remember, if you decide you don't like a particular area of stitching you can easily unpick and rework it in a different shade.)

Fill in the lines of the river and the central veins of the leaves in Back Stitches. Then work lines of Back Stitches radiating outwards from the centres of the star-like leaves, adding a central French Knot. On the smaller leaves scatter tiny Seeding Stitches. Work the small flower buds around the outer border as clusters of three French Knots to give a very rich texture.

Finally, outline the ducks in Back Stitches and then suggest detail with lines of Running Stitches and French Knots.

You will not be able to reproduce the exact colouring of the original cushion but will create your own personal interpretation of it.

7 When you have completed the embroidery, you are ready to stitch the narrow grey velvet ribbon around the central square. Find the tracing paper with the central square design and trim away the excess tracing paper around the design. Carefully pin this to the embroidery, aligning the design shapes as accurately as possible (you may find they vary slightly from paper to fabric). Use the edges of the paper transfer to guide you when pinning the velvet ribbon in position.

Allow a little spare ribbon at the first corner – your starting point. Carefully fold the ribbon to produce a mitred appearance at the next three corners. Do not try to push the pins through the layers and back up to the surface, simply stab them downwards to hold the ribbon in place. Leave the end of the ribbon loose at this stage.

Using matching grey sewing thread, hand-stitch the ribbon around the paper pattern working with tiny, invisible stitches along both edges of the ribbon and across the mitred folds at the three corners.

The corner where the ribbon starts and finishes requires careful attention as the ribbon is quite bulky and will fray once it is cut, but it does need to be neatened so that it looks identical to the other three corners. Trim the beginning of it (the underlying piece) straight across at the corner, but cut the end of it (the top piece) at an angle, allowing a small turning which you tuck under to hide the raw edge. Hand stitch this securely to hold it in position.

8 Find the other two pieces of tracing

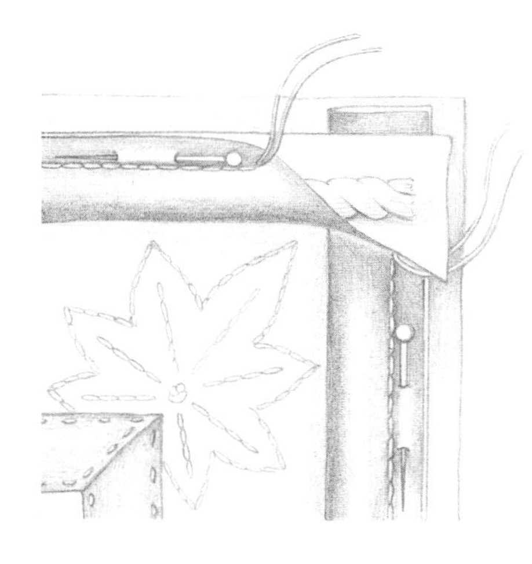

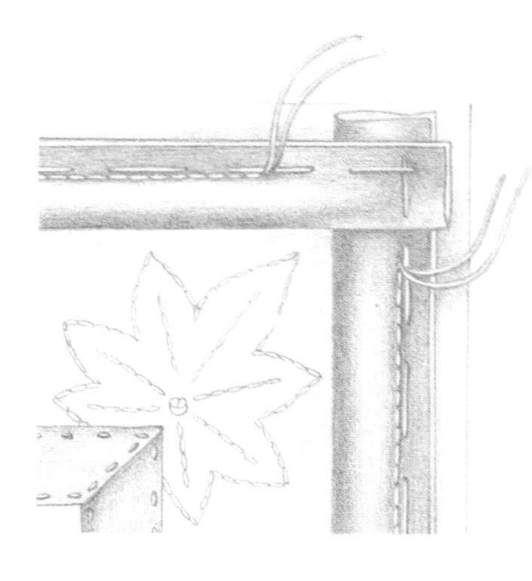

To neaten the ends of the velvet piping at the final corner first carefully unpick the stitching (top diagram) to allow you to snip across the piping inside the ribbon at the corner point, to reduce bulkiness. Then baste the piped ribbon across the corner point to neaten the edging and Machine Stitch to hold (bottom diagram).

paper with the transfer border patterns and cut around their outer edges. Pin them on to your cushion face, aligning them carefully as you did the central section. Baste around the trimmed edge of the paper to give you an accurately marked guideline to work along when applying the piped edging and also when making up the cushion.

9 Remove the paper patterns and then release the fabric from the frame.

Trim away the excess fabric leaving a 1.5 cm (⅝ in) seam allowance on all sides. (You will find that the heavily embroidered fabric wrinkles slightly when it is no longer held stretched and taut on the frame. Do not worry. Once the cushion is made up and filled the wrinkles will almost disappear, any that remain are not unattractive.)

10 Make the piped edging as follows. Fold the wide grey velvet ribbon around the piping cord and pinch the edges of the ribbon together. Then pin, baste and machine Straight Stitch along the edges as close as possible to the encased piping cord. (You will find it necessary to use a zip foot on your sewing machine when working with the piping cord.) Do not secure the loose threads at the ends of the piping.

11 Pin and baste the length of piping around the basted seam line of the embroidered cushion front. The piping must lie so that the edges of the ribbon face towards the cut edge of the fabric. Start and finish at one corner, turning the piping at the other three corners as sharply as possible. (You may find it necessary to snip the velvet ribbon edge towards the line of stitching at each corner point.)

The piping needs to be carefully neatened at the fourth corner where it starts and finishes as it is quite bulky and cannot be easily machined. Unpick the machine stitching at the ends of the piping so that you have access to the cord inside the velvet ribbon. Snip away the cord so that it does not overlap the corner point of the cushion front (the basted seam line), trim the ends of the velvet ribbon so that they overlap the corner by 1 cm (⅜ in). Baste the ribbon in position.

When you are satisfied that the piping is basted correctly along the seam line machine Straight Stitch it in place, keeping your stitching as close as possible to the ridge of the cord within the ribbon and inside your first line of machine stitching. Remove all basting threads.

12 Press the remaining square of linen-type fabric to remove any creases.

With right sides together place the cushion front over this square of fabric. Smooth the layers together and then carefully baste along the line of machine stitching that is holding the

piping in position. Machine stitch along this line of stitching remembering to leave an opening for the cushion pad. Trim away the excess fabric at the corners.

Turn to the right side and gently insert the cushion pad.

Using tiny Slip Stitches and a double length of sewing thread (for extra strength) hand sew along the open edges to close the gap and complete this beautiful cushion.

Although the Riverside Ducks Cushion and the Butterflies and Flowers Mirror Frame (see overleaf) use different techniques and are worked on a different scale, their colours and overall effect complement each other.

Butterflies and Flowers Mirror Frame

I worked this circular mirror frame on a fine linen-type fabric using pure cotton 'Nordin' yarns to give a matt result which is richly coloured and effective. The final finishing touch is the two-colour twisted cord around the inner and outer edges which enriches the frame and emphasises the turquoise and rust colours within the embroidered design.

The circular design is made up by repeating the quarter section motif which has a spray of flowers and foliage and a butterfly. The design could be adapted to make table mats by working on a coarser fabric using Coton Perlé or stranded threads. The butterfly could then be used as a single motif on drinks mats.

MATERIALS

Cream linen-type fabric, two pieces – 45 cm (18 in) square and 35 cm (14 in) square
White cotton fabric to back embroidery, 45 (18 in) square
Pelmet or heavyweight interfacing (Vilene), 30 cm (12 in) square Coats Nordin thread: 2 skeins Green 281; 1 skein each: Green 264, 269, 862, 215, Blue 150, 168, 928, Rust 778, 338, 341, Brown 277, 355, 365
Coats Soft Embroidery thread: 2 skeins each Rust 339, Blue 167
Rust or blue sewing thread to match Soft Embroidery thread
Cream sewing thread
Basting thread
Rigid cardboard to mount embroidery, 35 cm (14 in) square
2 curtain rings
Mirror, 25 cm (10 in) diameter, 3mm (1/8 in) thick
Fabric transfer pencil
Tracing paper, 35 cm (14 in) square
Strong multi-purpose clear adhesive glue
Sharp craft knife
Cutting mat or board
Wooden embroidery hoop, 35 cm (14 in) diameter or rectangular frame of suitable size

Stitches used: *Chain Stitch, French Knots, Buttonhole Stitch, Straight Stitch, Basting Stitch, Slip Stitch.*

TO MAKE THE MIRROR FRAME

1 Find and mark the centre of the sheet of tracing paper. Place this on top of the trace-off pattern of the design aligning the centre of the tracing paper with the marked centre point of the circular design segment.

Accurately trace the design on to the paper using the fabric transfer pencil and keeping as sharp a point as possible at all times. With a pencil or fine-tipped felt pen trace the broken lines on either side of the design to be used later as guidelines.

It is advisable to make a small test of the transfer pencil in one corner of the larger square of linen-type fabric to see how strong or faint the pencil marks are when transferred to the fabric.

Carefully reposition the tracing paper three more times over the trace-off pattern turning it each time around the centre point until your circular design is complete.

Press the larger piece of linen-type fabric to remove any creases.

Following the manufacturer's instructions, transfer the design centrally on to the right side of the fabric (also see page 135). You must be extremely careful not to move the paper during the process.

The transferred design will be a mirror image of the pattern on page 79. Reserve the tracing paper.

2 Press the white cotton fabric to

For this project I have used the fine matt cotton threads (Nordin) to achieve a delicate effect.

remove any creases and place it underneath the linen-type fabric aligning their edges.

3 Place the two layers of fabric centrally within the wooden embroidery hoop gently pulling the fabric around the hoop until it is taut and smooth within the inner working area.

If you are using a rectangular frame, stretch and fix the layers of fabric over the frame in the usual way, ensuring the straight grain of the fabric is parallel to the sides of the frame.

4 You are now ready to begin stitching. Use a single length of Nordin thread at all times and try to keep your stitches neat and even in size.

Follow the colour plan on page 79 to guide you when choosing the various shades of yarn. However this is not a strict plan and you may wish to adapt the colours so that the butterflies and sprays of flowers and foliage all vary slightly from one another. But if you do this you may use more of a particular shade than is recommended in the materials list.

The main stitch used is Chain Stitch, worked along the design lines of the leaves and stems of the foliage and the wings, body and antennae of the butterflies. Refer frequently to the

Opposite, Trace-off pattern for the mirror frame. The curved dotted lines indicate the seam lines. Remember to add a 2.5 cm (1") turning allowance outside this. Repeat this quarter section four times around the centre point to give a complete, circular design. Do not draw in the broken guidelines.

picture on page 77 and use it to help you build up the brown stems and fill in the pointed leaves with more lines of Chain Stitch, gradually changing the shades of green as required. The rounded leaves are not filled in with stitchery but are left with just a single line of Chain Stitches to give relief against the solid stitchery of the rest of the design.

Fill in the wings and body parts of the butterflies except for the centre areas of the lower wings (dark Green 862), the blue spots on the wings (Blue 168) and the centre parts of the body (Rust 341), which are all worked in tiny French Knots. Work the knots close to each other to produce a massed area of knotty texture. The eyes are also worked in French Knots.

Work the centre of the large, open flower in French Knots to give a rich texture, then around it work small Straight Stitches of dark blue and mid-blue. Around these stitches work closely-spaced Buttonhole Stitches in light blue so that the bars of the stitches form a neatly raised edge to each petal. The smaller flower buds are worked in Buttonhole Stitch.

5 When you have completed the stitchery, find the tracing paper with the design (from step 1). Trim away the excess paper around the outer broken line (guideline) of the transfer design and also from within the centre of it to give a template of the mirror frame. Place this over the stitchery, aligning the drawn shapes with the embroidered shapes, and pin to hold. Accurately baste around the paper pattern to give the approximate position of the inner and outer edges of the frame.

6 Remove the paper template and release the fabric from the frame. Trim away the excess fabric leaving 2.5 cm (1 in) all around the outer edge.

7 Cut out a circle measuring 28 cm (11 in) diameter from the cardboard. Then cut out a central circle measuring 17 cm (6¾ in) diameter.

Place the embroidery face downwards on a clean, flat surface and place the cardboard frame over it, so that the circular frame lies centrally over the fabric.

Using a pair of sharp-pointed trimming scissors snip the fabric allowance in towards the outer edge of the frame. Then fold the allowance over the edge of the frame and push dressmakers' pins through the fabric and into the edge of the cardboard to hold the embroidery in position. At this stage you can check that your frame is correctly positioned and make any adjustments that are necessary. When you are satisfied that you have stretched and pinned the fabric around the frame effectively, use the glue to hold the turned fabric to the wrong side of the cardboard frame. (Follow the manufacturer's instructions when using the glue.) Do not remove the pins at this point but leave them in position until the glue has thoroughly dried.

Using the sharp-pointed scissors cut away the central area of the fabric leaving the same turning allowance as before (2.5 cm or 1 in). Snip in towards the inner edge of the cardboard and repeat the process of turning, pinning and gluing the fabric to the wrong side of the inner edge of the cardboard.

When the fabric is firmly glued in position carefully remove the pins.

8 Make the backing of the mirror frame by cutting a circle measuring 28 cm (11 in) diameter from the heavyweight interfacing. Place this over the remaining square of linen-type fabric. Pin to hold the layers together before trimming away the excess fabric leaving a small turning of 1.5 cm (⅝ in). Snip the fabric towards the edge of the interfacing before turning and basting the allowance to hold. Do not let your basting stitches show on the right side of the backing shape as these stitches will remain permanently in position.

778
338
341
355
365
277
281
862
264
215
269
928
168
150

Hand-stitch the two curtain rings to the right side of the backing shape. These will be used for hanging the mirror.

9 Use the skeins of Soft Embroidery thread to make a two-colour twisted cord. Use six lengths of each colour, carefully dividing each skein of the two colours into three equal lengths (see Special Techniques page 138).

Using either matching blue or rust sewing thread (a double length for extra strength), carefully sew the cord around the inner and outer edges of the frame. You will have to be extremely careful when securing the ends of the cord as it will unravel once cut unless held tightly.

To neaten the cord and make it appear continuous allow a little extra cord than is needed and let this unravel slightly so that the individual threads can be passed through the edge of the fabric to the wrong side of the frame using a large-eyed needle. If you are patient and careful you will achieve a very neat edging.

10 Finally, with wrong sides together stitch the front and back of the mirror frame together using a double length of cream sewing thread. Before stitching all the way round the frame carefully slip the mirror in between the layers. Continue stitching the edges together to enclose the mirror.

Butterflies and Flowers Towel

The strong green colour of the towel complements the vividly bright border which decorates it. The design source of this delightful project is a faded and rather frayed example of a Chinese sleeve band that would have once been attached to a robe or coat. I purchased it some years ago in Lymington, Hampshire in the street market for a few shillings. The wrong side of the sleeve band shows the intensity of the original colouring and it is these colours that have been my inspiration for the towel border.

MATERIALS

Jade-green cotton lawn, 40 × 70 cm (16 × 28 in)
Green hand towel to complement cotton lawn, width 56 cm (22 in)
Coats Anchor stranded embroidery thread: 1 skein each Green 256, 238, 187, 204, Brown 905, 832, 942, Cream 275, Pink 40, 24, 271, Magenta 90, 87, Lavender 117, 118
Fabric transfer pencil
Strip of tracing paper approximately 10 × 60 cm (4 × 24 in)
Piece of tracing paper, A4 size
Fine-tipped black felt pen
Sewing thread to match cotton lawn
Tailor's chalk or dressmaker's pencil
Basting thread
15 cm (6 in) wooden embroidery hoop

Stitches used: *Diagonal Basting Stitch, Satin Stitch, French Knots, Back Stitch, machine Straight Stitch, machine Satin Stitch, machine Zigzag Stitch, Slip Stitch.*

TO MAKE THE BORDER

1 Trace the design on to the A4 piece of tracing paper using the felt pen to make lines which are clearly seen as you will use both sides of the tracing paper to produce your repeat pattern for the border.

2 Draw the parallel guidelines along either side of the design. Then draw two parallel lines along the length of the strip of tracing paper so that they are 7.5 cm (3 in) apart. These will help you align the repeat pattern accurately in a straight line.

3 Place the traced design under one end of the long strip of paper. Tape the layers to a smooth, flat working surface (white is ideal) to prevent any movement, then begin drawing the design carefully on to the strip with the fabric transfer pencil. Do not draw the parallel lines with the pencil.

Always work with a fine point to your pencil so that you produce as thin a line as possible. You will find it worthwhile to draw a few test lines on a spare piece of tracing paper and then transfer them to a scrap of similar fabric to the one you are about to use as you will then see how strong or weak the transfer lines are and can adjust how much pressure you apply to the pencil.

When you have drawn the first repeat section, release the pieces of paper. Turn the original traced design over so that it becomes reversed and position it under the long strip close to the section you have just drawn so that the shapes fit together. Trace the design on to the strip with the transfer pencil. Repeat this process once more, turning the design back over to its original position to draw the third section.

NB: If you are making a longer order strip for a wider towel simply keep repeating the sections, remember to reverse the design for every other section.

4 Fold the jade-green cotton lawn in half lengthways to give a long strip of double thickness. Press to flatten it and remove any creases.

5 Place the paper design strip with the transfer facing downwards centrally along the double layer of fabric and with your pre-heated iron carefully transfer the design to the fabric (follow the pencil manufacturer's instructions carefully). You must be extremely careful not to move the paper during this process or you will cause a blurred and distorted image to be ironed on to the fabric. Reserve the transfer strip.

6 Work two lines of Diagonal Basting Stitches along the fabric strip to hold the two layers together. Place one end of the fabric strip in the hoop and pull it gently to give a taut working area. Reposition the hoop as necessary while you are working the border pattern.

7 Use three strands of embroidery at all times unless otherwise directed.

8 There is no definite colour sequence to follow but try to select the colours carefully balancing them against one another as you build up the design. Look closely at the detail overleaf to see how to use the colours. The Green shades are for the leaves, the Browns and Cream are for the butterflies and the Pinks, Magentas and Lavenders are for the flowers.

Most of the design is worked in Satin Stitch with only isolated French

275
942
832
905
187
204
238
256
271
24
40
90
87
117
118

Knots and some Back Stitches to embellish the brown butterflies.

You will find that the Satin Stitches will sometimes overlap one another if you are working from a small area outwards into a larger area and vice versa. Remember that, as its names implies, it is indeed a Satin Stitch giving the smooth and even effect of satin fabric and cannot therefore bend to fit a shape. However, by carefully selecting which direction in which to lay your stitches you will fill a complicated shape and give the appearance of curved stitchery within it.

Use the light and dark shades of Magenta and Lavender together with combinations of light and mid-Pink or mid- and dark Pink to work the small flowers. All three shades of Pink are required to work the largest of the full blooms working from the deepest shade on the outer edges to the pale shade at its heart. With all the flowers fill each petal shape so that the Satin Stitches appear to be growing upwards from the base of the flower or outwards from its centre.

When working the second shade of any flower do not stop this line of stitching at the same place as the first line. Instead work a little over the first line to give a graded effect like Encroaching Satin Stitch. It does not matter if your needle splits a previous stitch providing the effect is pleasing to the eye.

The leaves are also worked in Satin Stitches. Select your shade of Green thread to give a balanced design. Do not use a lot of one shade and forget the others, use them all throughout the border strip. Always work the Satin Stitches so that they are pointing towards the leaf tips as this will give a pleasing effect. The right choice of position for the Satin Stitches is important to order to make the leaves look effective.

Finally the butterflies are worked in a combination of the Brown shades and Cream. Each butterfly can be worked slightly differently in its colour pattern. Using Satin Stitch, work vertically along the length of the body and then radiate outwards for the semi-circular lower wings and in a fan-like direction for the upper wings. When working the lower wings the Satin Stitches can encroach upon one another but for the upper wings and body the shape of each coloured row of stitches is clearly defined.

Work the antennae in small, neat, dark Brown Back Stitches. Then, using only two strands of dark Green (187), work a tiny French Knot at the centres of the lower wings and in each 'eye' of the upper wings. Work tiny Back Stitch lines to decorate the upper wings, using the trace-off pattern as a guide. You will have to work these

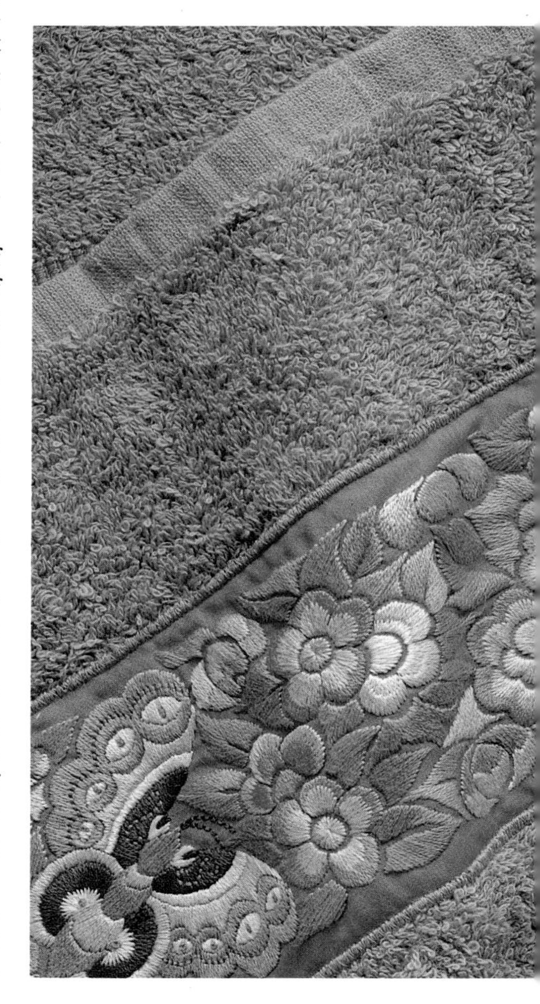

lines by eye as you will have covered the transfer markings with your Satin Stitches. If you are unsatisfied with your Back Stitches you can easily unpick a few stitches and rework them.

9 When you have completed the embroidery remove it from the hoop. The fabric will need to be carefully pressed on the wrong side to remove all the creases caused during handling. Use a steam iron or a dry iron with a damp cloth.

10 Trim the reserved transfer strip along the parallel guidelines and place the strip over the embroidery aligning the drawn design with the embroidered shapes. Using tailor's chalk or a dressmaker's pencil mark the edges of the border on to the fabric.

Using matching thread, machine Satin Stitch along each drawn line (set the stitch width to 3 mm or ⅛ in).

Carefully cut away the surplus fabric on the outside edge of the satin stitching. Pin the border across one end of the hand towel (covering the decorative woven line if there is one). Trim the raw ends of the strip leaving 1 cm (⅜ in) turning allowance and tuck this in to neaten.

With Zigzag Stitch at a width of 3 mm (⅛ in), machine along the satin-stitch edges. The Zigzag Stitches will merge into the Satin Stitches while firmly attaching the border to the towel.

By hand, work tiny Slip Stitches along the turned in ends of the border to complete this beautiful hand towel.

Refer to this close-up photograph when following the trace-off pattern and colour stitch guide on page 81. It will help you to follow the stitch directions shown on the trace-off pattern.

WILD CAT CUSHION

The style of this striking cushion is very like that of the Riverside Ducks Cushion (see pages 68–75) with fabric dye crayons and back stitching being used to great effect. The techniques used are quite quick and produce a rich and very pleasing result. The use of velvet ribbons adds the final touches to produce this eye-catching design.

The cushion is one of the easiest in this book and even if you are relatively inexperienced with a needle you should find this quick and straightforward to work. It goes well with the Riverside Ducks cushion on page 68, should you wish to make a pair of cushions. The crayon technique is easy to master, and is also used for the Shell and Fish table mats on page 12 and the Prunus Blossom Box on page 16.

MATERIALS

Cream linen-type fabric with a rough weave, two pieces – 56 cm (22 in) square and 42 cm (16½ in) square
White cotton backing fabric, 56 cm (22 in) square
Sage-green velvet ribbon, 1 cm (⅜ in) wide and 1.4 m (1½ yd) long
Sage-green velvet ribbon, 1.5 cm (⅝ in) wide and 1.85 m (2 yd) long
No 2 piping cord, 1.85 m (2 yd) long
Green sewing thread to match velvet ribbon
Basting thread
Crayola fabric transfer dye crayons
Coats Soft Embroidery cotton thread, 2 skeins Green 217; 1 skein each Green 213, 255, 267, Rust 337, 349, Pink 894, 895, Gold 307, Blue 168, 170, 837, 850, Grey 815
Cushion pad, 40 cm (16 in) square
Tracing paper, 3 sheets A3 size
Layout paper, 1 sheet A3 size
Wooden frame, 50 cm (20 in) square
Fine-tipped black felt pen

213
255
267
217
307
337
349
170
168
850
894
895
815
837

centre

position of velvet ribbon

213
255
267
217
307
337
349
170
168
850
894
895
815
837

Stitches used: *Back Stitch, French Knots, Slip Stitch, machine Straight Stitch.*

TO MAKE THE CUSHION

1 Using the sheet of layout paper enlarge the central square section of the design on page 85, doubling it in size so that it measures 26 cm (10¼ in) square. You can do this by drawing a square of this size and then dividing it up equally into sixteen smaller squares each measuring 6.5 cm (2⅗ in). Then transfer the design on to this grid, enlarging it with the aid of the grid lines (see Special Techniques page 133). Alternatively, if you have access to a photocopier that can enlarge and reduce material then you can easily and quickly enlarge the design to the correct size, i.e. to 26 cm (10¼ in) square.

Once you have enlarged the design trace it accurately, using the felt pen, on to one of the sheets of tracing paper.

2 Trace the corner section of the border on to one half of a second sheet of tracing paper, positioning it so that you can then draw a second corner section next to it to form one half of the border. Then trace both these adjoining corner sections on to the remaining sheet of tracing paper to produce the second half of the border. (Use the centre section if necessary to ensure the border fits accurately around it.)

3 Following the manufacturer's instructions (also see Special Techniques page 135), make a test strip of the different colours which can be achieved with the dye crayons. (Position your test strip along one edge of the larger square of the linen-type fabric.) Remember that you can blend the crayons and vary their strength of colour.

Use the crayons to colour in the underside of the tracing paper with the two half border sections and the inner square. Refer closely to the finished cushion (see page 84) to help you choose your colours. Looking at the shades of the Soft Embroidery threads will also help you. The overall colouring is quite soft so you will not need to press very hard with the crayons as this would produce very strong colours.

4 Press the larger piece of cream linen-type fabric to remove any creases. Once more following the manufacturer's instructions carefully transfer the square design on to the centre of the fabric aligning the sides of the design with the straight grain of the fabric. Remember to place the transfer waxy side down on the fabric and take great care not to move the transfer when you use the iron as any movement will create a blurred image.

Place one half of the border transfer in position, aligning the broken guide-lines of the border around the central square. Double-check it is correctly positioned before applying the iron to it.

Repeat this process with the second half of the border.

Reserve the three pieces of tracing paper – you will need them when finishing the cushion.

5 Stretch the white cotton backing fabric and then the linen-type fabric on the wooden frame, making sure the crayonned design is centrally positioned and that the straight grain of the fabric is parallel to the sides of the frame.

6 You are now ready to work the embroidery. Use neat and even Back Stitches to outline all the design shapes allowing the colour changes of the crayonning to influence your choice of thread colour. Also refer to the photograph on page 84 to guide you.

The small circle markings of the trace-off pattern which are found in the wild cat's body and also on the flowers and large leaves of the border design are worked in French Knots to give a raised and rich texture.

With this type of design which relies heavily on the colouring created by the use of the dye crayons it is important to remember that the colour guide

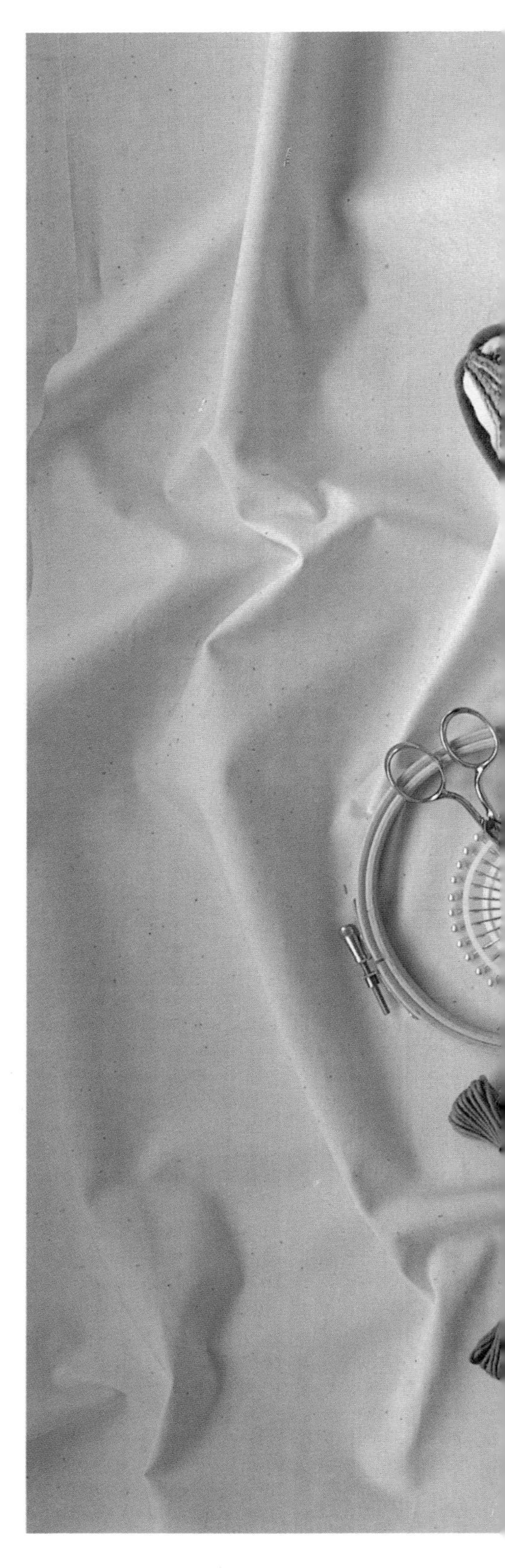

does not have to be followed exactly. If you feel the colouring of the transferred design would be enhanced by a different shade of thread then feel confident enough to experiment and choose your own colour scheme.

7 When you have completed the embroidery you are ready to stitch the narrow green velvet ribbon around the central square. Find the tracing paper with the central square design and trim away all the excess tracing paper around the broken guidelines of the design. Pin this to the embroidery, aligning the design shapes as accurately as possible (you may find they vary slightly from paper to embroidery). Use the edges of the paper transfer to guide you when pinning the ribbon in position.

Allow a little spare ribbon at the first corner – your starting point. Carefully fold the ribbon to produce a mitred appearance at the next three corners. Do not try to push the pins through all the layers and back up to the surface, simply stab then downwards to hold the ribbon in place. Leave the end of the ribbon loose at this stage.

Using matching green sewing thread, hand-stitch the ribbon around the paper pattern working with tiny, invisible stitches along both edges of the ribbon and across the mitred folds at the three corners.

The corner where the ribbon starts and finishes requires careful attention as the ribbon is quite bulky and will fray once it is cut, but it does need to be neatened so that it looks identical to the other three corners. Trim the beginning of it (the underlying piece) straight across at the outer edge of the corner, but cut the other end of it at an angle, allowing a small turning which you tuck under to hide the raw edge. Hand-stitch this securely in position.

8 Find the other two pieces of tracing paper with the transfer border patterns and cut around their outer edges. Pin them on your cushion face, aligning them carefully as you did the central section. Baste around the edge of the paper to give you an accurately marked guideline to work along when applying the piped edging and also when making up the cushion.

9 Remove the paper patterns and then release the fabric from the frame.

Trim away the excess fabric leaving a 1.5 cm (⅝ in) seam allowance on all sides.

(You will find that the embroidered fabric wrinkles slightly when it is no longer held taut on the frame. Do not worry about this. Once the cushion is made up and filled the wrinkles will almost disappear, any that remain are not unattractive to the eye.)

10 Make the piped edging as follows. Fold the wide green velvet ribbon around the piping cord and pinch the edges of the ribbon together. Then pin, baste and machine Straight Stitch

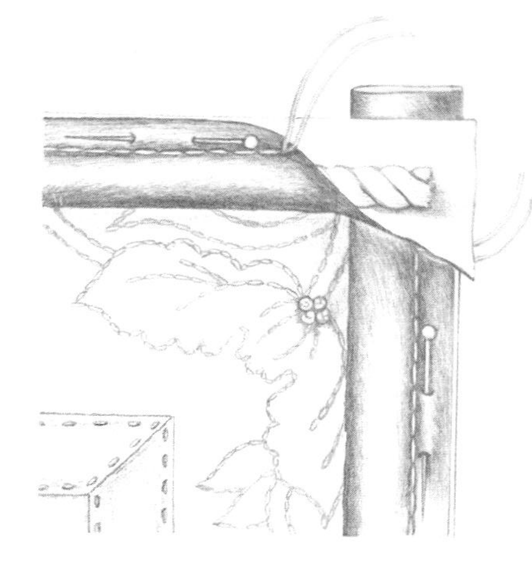

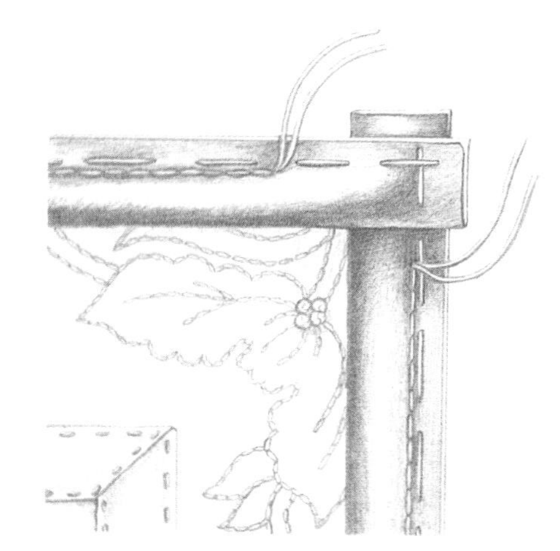

To neaten the ends of the velvet piping at the final corner first carefully unpick the stitching (near right diagram) to allow you to snip across the piping inside the ribbon at the corner point, to reduce bulkiness. Then baste the piped ribbon across the corner point to neaten the edging and Machine Stitch to hold (far right diagram).

along the edges as close as possible to the encased piping cord. (You will find it necessary to use a zip foot on your sewing machine when working with the piping cord.) Do not secure the loose threads at the ends of the piping.

11 Pin and baste the length of piping around the basted seam line of the embroidered cushion front. The piping must lie so that the edges of the ribbon lie facing towards the cut edge of the fabric. Start and finish at one corner, turning the piping at the other three corners as sharply as possible. (You may find it necessary to snip the velvet ribbon edge towards the line of stitching at each corner point.)

The piping needs to be carefully neatened at the fourth corner where it starts and finishes as it is quite bulky and cannot be machined easily. Unpick the machine stitching at the ends of the piping so that you have access to the cord inside the velvet ribbon. Snip away the cord so that it does not overlap the corner point of the cushion front (the basted seam line). Trim the ends of the velvet ribbon so that they overlap the corner by 1 cm (3/8 in). Baste the ribbon in position.

When you are satisfied that the piping is basted correctly along the seam line, machine Straight Stitch it in place, keeping your stitching as close as possible to the ridge of the cord within the ribbon and inside your first line of machine stitching. Remove all the basting threads.

12 Press the remaining square of linen-type fabric to remove any creases.

With right sides together place the cushion front over this square of fabric. Smooth the layers together and then carefully baste along the line of machine stitching that is holding the piping in position.

Machine stitch along this line of stitching remembering to leave an opening for the cushion pad. Trim away the excess fabric at the corners.

Carefully fold the velvet ribbon at each corner to produce a neat mitred corner, as shown above.

Turn to the right side and gently insert the cushion pad. Using tiny Slip Stitches and a double length of sewing thread (for extra strength) hand-sew along the open edges to close the gap and complete your Wild Cat cushion.

An interesting adaption of this design would be to work just the central square section and then frame it to make a delightful wall picture. You could follow the same techniques and colour scheme of the cushion or you might like to vary them to produce a different result. Always try out any new techniques, stitches or colourways and critically assess them before working them too much on your piece of embroidery. Remember that with most methods of stitchery you always unpick and re-work an area that you are not pleased with.

Lucky Bats and Gourds Sewing Roll and Pin Cushion

This delightful canvaswork sewing roll has a hidden pocket and a series of elasticated loops in which sewing threads, embroidery yarns, scissors, needles and other notions can be safely held. The matching pin cushion can also be kept in the roll.

The bold colouring and striking design was inspired by a small porcelain bowl of Chinese origin, dated between 1723–35. The motifs of the original design are simple and are repeated around the elegant shape of the bowl. Green swirling clouds are seen on a clear yellow background. Flying between the clouds are several small red bats; each bat is holding a gourd vase suspended from trailing blue ribbons. The bats are symbols of luck because of the happiness they bring. The word for bat is 'fu' in Chinese and is pronounced in the same way as the word for happiness, hence the link.

MATERIALS

White mono canvas (15 holes per in), 33 × 63 cm (13 × 25 in)
Bright-green glazed cotton fabric, 30 × 90 cm (12 × 36 in)
Elastic, 6 mm (¼ in) wide and 50 cm (20 in) long
Pelmet or heavyweight interfacing (Vilene), 22 × 36 cm (8½ × 14 in)
Coats tapisserie wool: 6 skeins Yellow 0305; 3 skeins each Blue 0123, Red 013, Green 0265; 2 skeins each Green 0257, 3150, 0203, 0243; 1 skein each Blue 0121, 0167, Red 0412
Sewing thread to match green glazed cotton fabric
Sewing thread to match either Red 013 or Blue 0123
Basting thread
1 clear plastic press stud
Small amount of terylene or polyester filling
Tracing paper
Squared paper (optional)
Wooden frame, 30 × 60 cm (12 × 24 in)
Waterproof marking pen

Stitches used: *Tent Stitch, Diagonal Basting Stitch, machine Straight Stitch, Slip Stitch.*

TO MAKE THE SEWING ROLL AND PIN CUSHION

Reserve one skein of Red 013 and Blue 0123 to make the twisted cord later (step 10).

1 Stretch the canvas on to the frame ensuring the threads of the canvas are parallel to the sides of the frame. Within this working space you will have room for both the sewing roll design and the small square of the pin cushion. Count across the width of the stretched canvas to find the centre thread. Lightly mark this centre thread along the length of the canvas using the waterproof marking pen. This will act as a guideline to help you position the sewing roll design upon the canvas and it is also helpful to use the line to check that you are working accurately from chart to canvas; it is surprisingly easy to jump a square or a stitch.

2 At the centre guideline measure 4 cm (1½ in) from the inner edge of the wooden frame to find where you shall start working the sewing roll design. This will give you plenty of room at the other end of the stretched canvas to work the pin cushion design once the sewing roll design is complete. Work carefully and methodically, following the chart on pages 94–5.

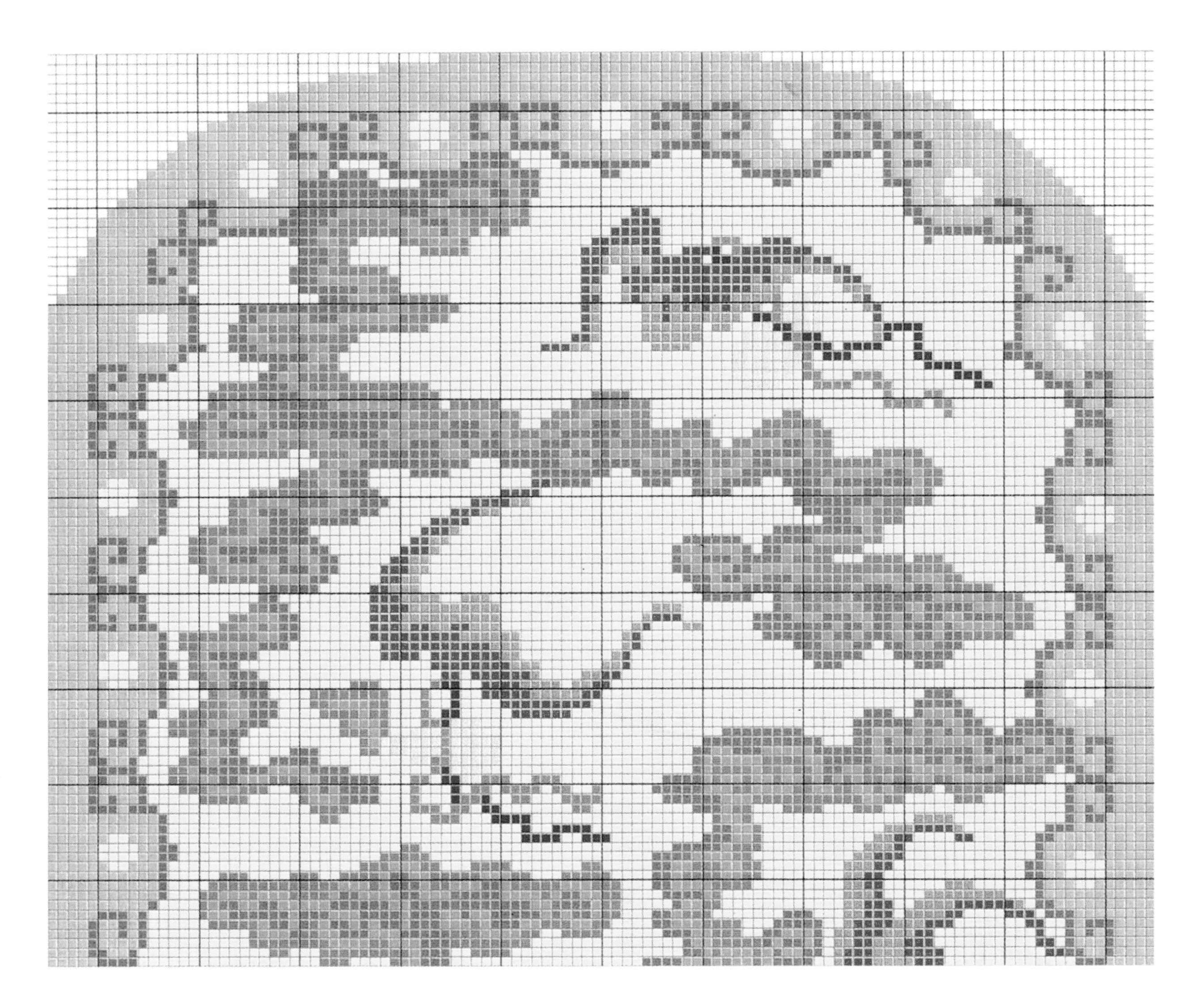

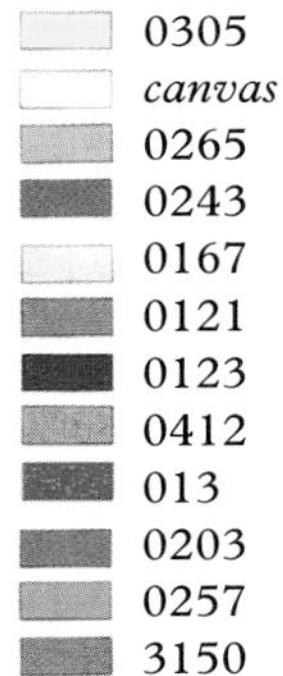

Each square on the chart represents a single Tent Stitch which is worked over one horizontal and one vertical thread of canvas (i.e. one intersection).

Begin your stitchery at the centre guideline. You may find it beneficial to work some of the dark Green 0243 pattern to begin with as this will quickly give you a framework around which you can then fill in the rest of the design.

All the Tent Stitches must be worked in the same direction for a smooth and even effect. Always work as economically as possible with your yarn. Do not take your yarn across the back of the canvas from one area to another unless they are very close; finish off and start again for a neater result. Do not use very long lengths of yarn as the wool is easily worn thin by the repeated action of passing it backwards and forwards through the rough canvas.

When filling in the larger background areas of yellow try to work methodically across the canvas building up your stitchery either horizontally or vertically in yellow areas. This will produce a smooth and even background area whereas if you work erratically across, down and diagonally over the canvas the effect will be quite uneven.

3 When you have completed the stitchery of the sewing roll shape then you can work the smaller square design of the pin cushion. Measure and leave a space of 6 cm (2½ in) between the edge of the sewing roll design and the edge of the pin cushion design. You can position the pin cushion square over towards one corner if you wish. Work this edge first to be assured that the two designs will not clash on the canvas.

Work the design in the same way as the sewing roll following the chart on page 97.

4 When you have completed all the stitchery remove the canvas from the frame. Trim away the excess canvas leaving a 1 cm (⅜ in) allowance of bare canvas on all sides of both pieces of canvaswork. (The larger pieces of excess canvas can be saved and used for working trial stitches etc., for other projects.)

5 Make the sewing roll.

Enlarge the half section of the outline shape of the sewing roll (see page 98 and its caption). Trace it on to half of a large sheet of tracing paper, then reposition the paper over the shape aligning the dotted lines and trace it once more so that you now have the complete shape of the roll. Carefully cut this out to become your template.

Press the green fabric to remove any creases.

This sewing roll chart is shown in two halves but should be worked as one continuous piece. Work the top half then follow on with the bottom half.

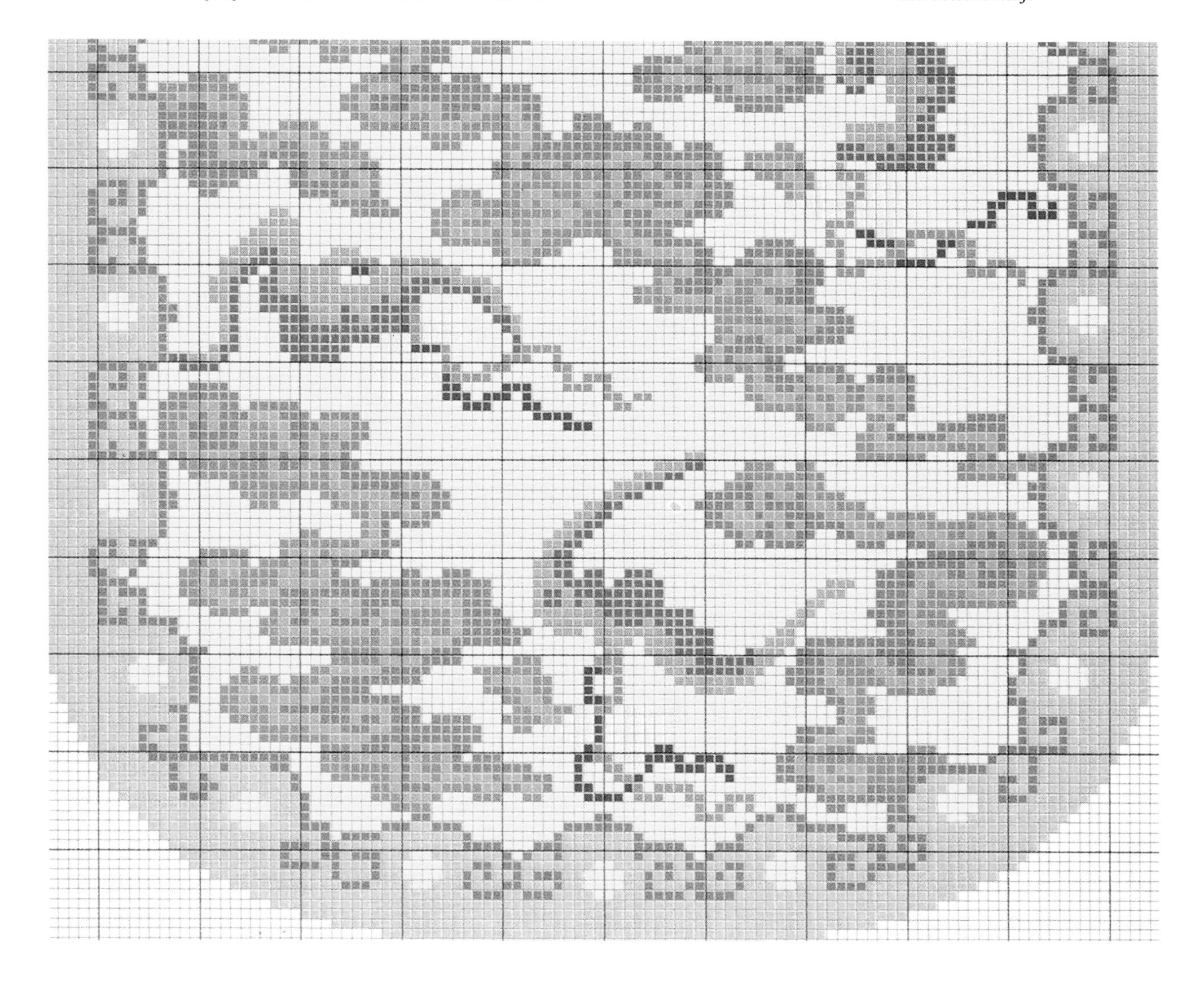

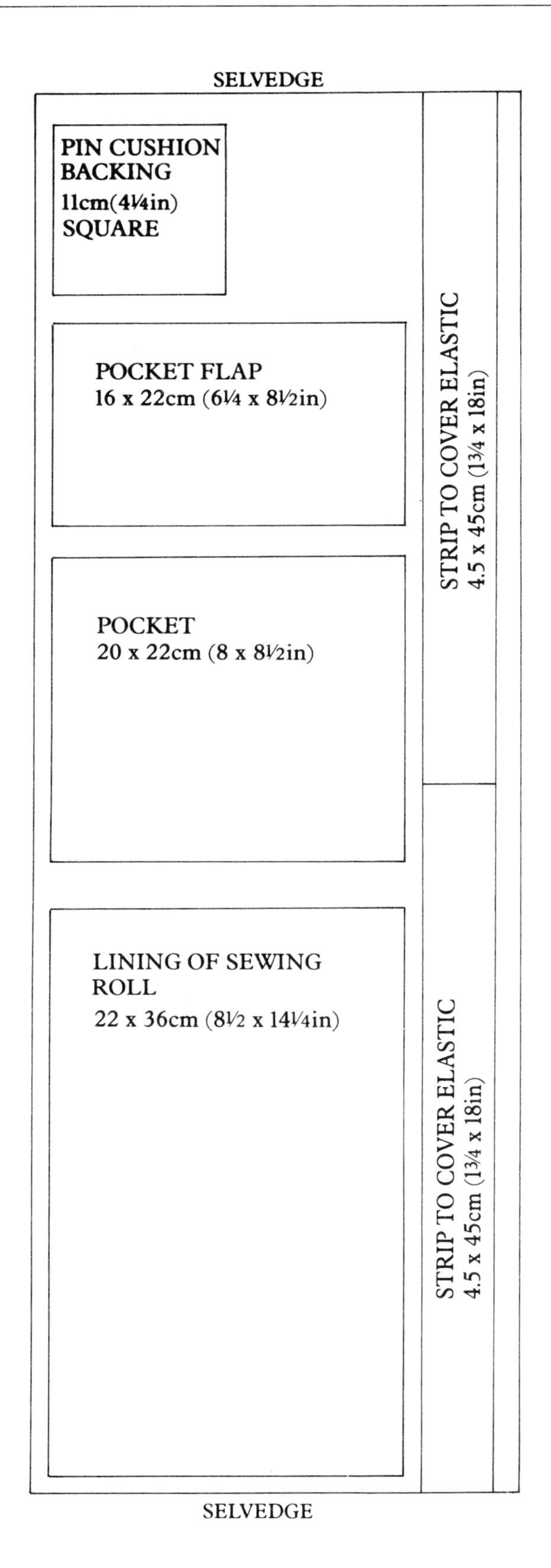

Follow the cutting guide on the left to cut out the green glazed cotton. (Reserve the small square piece to be used for the pin cushion.) Cut the shapes so that their edges are parallel to the straight grain of the fabric.

You may prefer to make paper patterns for each shape from squared paper and place these on the fabric rather than simply measuring and then cutting the fabric.

6 With wrong sides together baste the pelmet-weight interfacing to the large piece of green lining fabric, smoothing the two pieces together so that their edges match. Use Diagonal Basting Stitches to make sure the layers lay flat against one another (see Special Techniques page 137). Then pin the sewing roll template centrally on the green fabric and with small stitches baste around the edge of the template so that its shape is accurately transferred to the lining fabric. This line will become your seam line when you make up the sewing roll.

7 Make the pocket flap.

With right sides together fold the pocket flap piece in half so that it measures 8×22 cm (3¼ ×8½ in). Place the paper template of the sewing roll over the folded fabric so that one of the curved ends lies towards the raw edges of the fabric.

Adjust the template so that it is centrally positioned between the two short ends and measures 6.5 cm (2½ in) from the folded edge of the fabric to the edge of the template. Pin the template in position and accurately baste around its edges. Remove the template then, with your sewing machine set to Straight Stitch and using matching thread, work a seam around the basted line, leaving a small opening at one end of your seam line.

Trim away the surplus fabric and snip the seam allowance in towards the line of stitching.

Turn the pocket flap to the right side and gently ease it into an evenly curved flat shape. Press it carefully

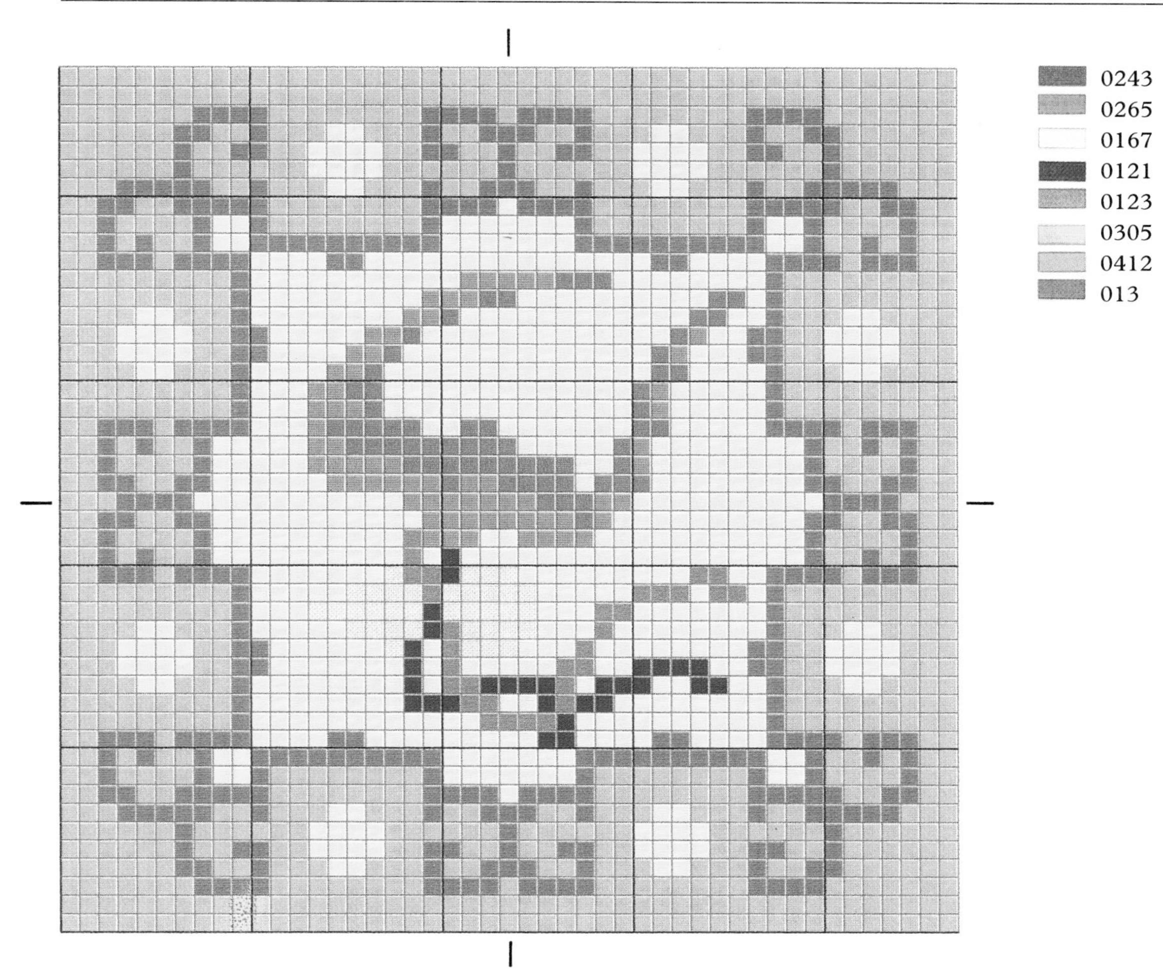

with a steam iron, tucking in the raw edges of the opening, and Slip Stitch the edges together to close.

Work a double line of top stitching around the curved edge of the pocket flap to neaten and decorate.

8 Make the pocket.

With right sides outside, fold the remaining rectangle of green fabric in half so that the double layer measures 10×22 cm (4×8½ in). Along the folded straight edge work a double line of top stitching to decorate (similar to that of the pocket flap). If you wish you can add further lines of top stitching to decorate the pocket.

Place the paper template over the pocket piece as you did for the flap, centring the template between the short sides and allowing 9 cm (3½ in) from the folded edge of the fabric to the curved edge of the template. Pin the

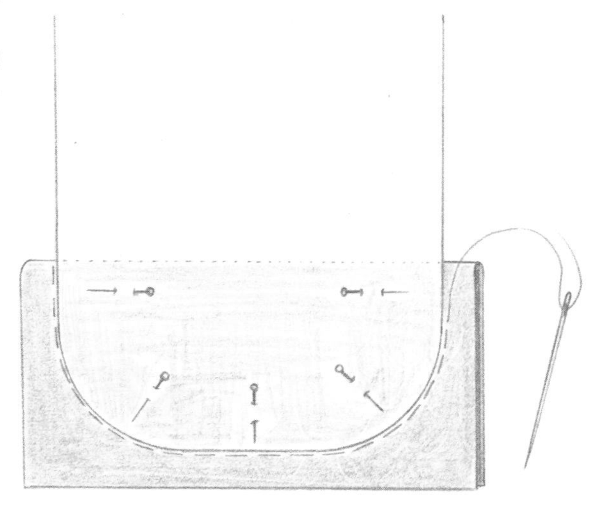

Above, Cutting out and preparing the pocket flap (see Step 7); opposite, cutting plan for the green cotton fabric.

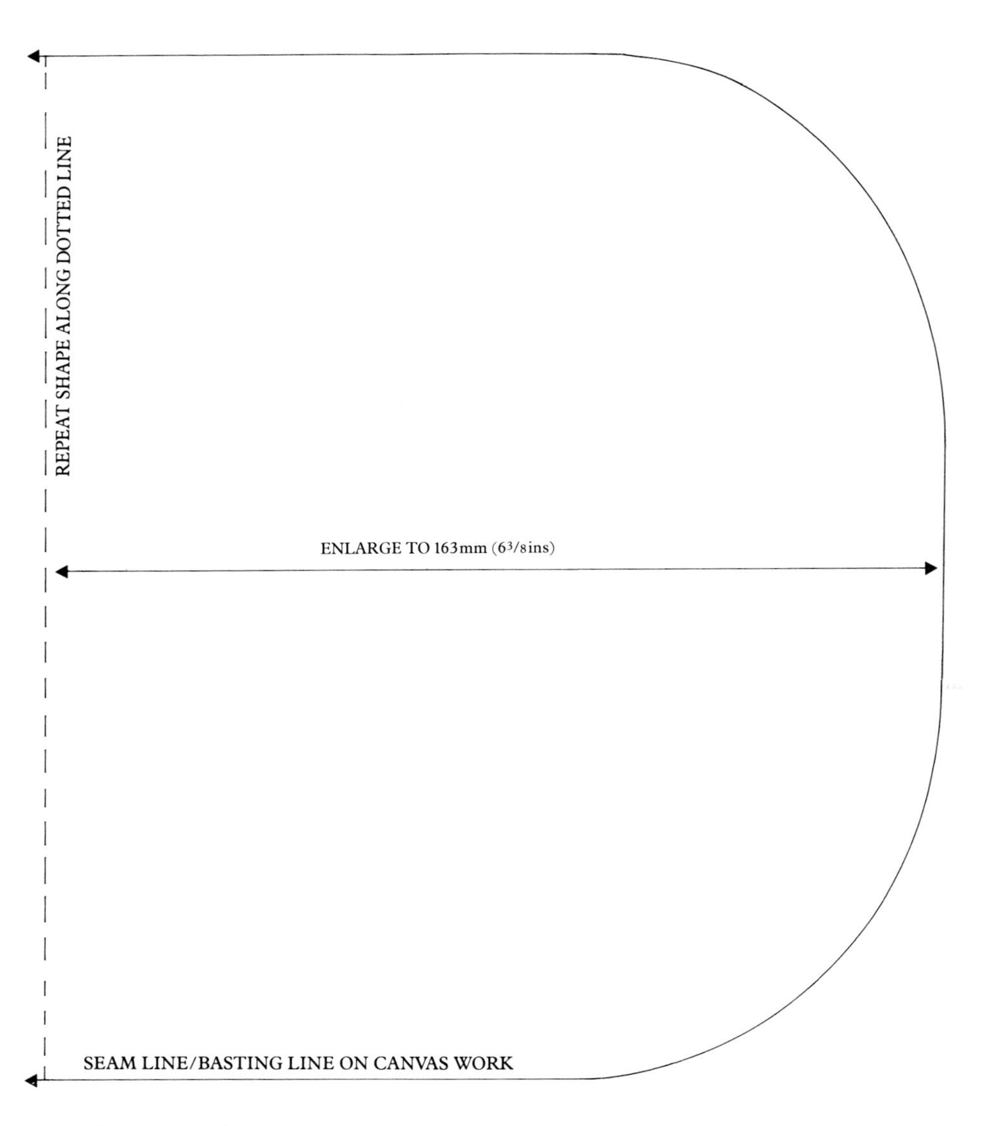

Enlarge this diagram of the sewing roll shape by 135% before making your template (see page 133). The final depth should be 192 mm (7½").

template to hold, and baste around the curved shape. Remove the template and trim away the surplus fabric but leave a 1 cm (⅜ in) seam allowance.

Place the lining shape green side uppermost on a clean, flat surface. Place the pocket piece at one end of the larger shape, matching up the basted seam lines. Pin and baste the layers together before machine Straight Stitching around the sides and base of the pocket piece.

9 Make the elasticated strips.

With right sides together fold each strip in half and machine Straight Stitch along the long raw edges taking only a narrow seam allowance. Then carefully turn each strip to the right side. This is quite difficult to do as the strips are narrow but it can be made easier by pinning a small safety pin through one layer of the fabric at the end of the strip. Then push the safety pin inside the strip, gently easing it in; as you push it further and further you will find that it takes the strip inside with it. When the pin emerges at the other end keep on pulling and you will see the strip turn inside out and end up with its right side facing outwards.

Carefully press each strip with the seam along one edge. Then top stitch along the strips, working close to each edge. Make sure you leave enough space for the elastic to be threaded through the centre of the strip.

Cut the elastic in half. Use the safety pin to thread each piece into a fabric strip. Pin the elastic at each end of the fabric strip to hold it firmly in place. Arrange the two strips on the sewing roll lining, spacing them evenly apart. Pin their ends in position before machine Straight Stitching them firmly to the lining.

Decide how many elasticated loops you want and how they are to be spaced apart. Then baste to mark each division before securely machine Straight Stitching the strips at the chosen positions.

Place the pocket flap near to the pocket so that its straight edge will cover and hide the raw ends of the strips. Pin and baste it in position and then carefully work a double line of machine Straight Stitching along the edge.

10 Make up the sewing roll.
Carefully position the template on the right side of the canvaswork shape and accurately baste around it to give you a seam line.

With right sides together pin and baste the canvaswork shape to the lining so that the pocket of the lining is at the top end of the canvaswork design. You will have to match up the two shapes carefully and patiently and you may find that you need to pull the canvaswork a little to get it into the correct shape.

Machine Straight Stitch around the shape leaving an opening along one of the straight sides. Check that your line of stitching is correct before trimming away the excess fabric and clip in towards the seam at the curves.

Very carefully ease the roll inside out and gently pull and smooth into shape. If necessary press to flatten into shape. Tuck in the raw edges of the opening and close this with tiny Slip Stitches.

Fold the roll in three, with the pocket innermost, and decide where you want to stitch the press stud. Then securely hand-sew the two halves of the press stud in position. Use green thread to sew one half on to the green lining fabric and, if possible, use a matching coloured thread to sew the other half on to the canvaswork to blend with the area you stitch it to.

Finally, make a length of two-coloured twisted cord using the reserved skeins of red and blue tapisserie wools. Cut three lengths of blue and three lengths of red yarn, each length measuring 2.5m (2¾ yd). To make the cord see Special Techniques page 138.

Slip Stitch the cord around the sewing roll, beginning at the centre of the top curved edge (where the press stud lies). Leave enough cord at the beginning to tie into a neat bow with the remainder of the cord. Knot the cord ends before trimming the excess and teasing out the loose ends to make fake tassels. Tie the end of the surplus cord quickly once you have cut it to prevent it unravelling. You will need this to stitch around the pin cushion.

11 Make the pin cushion.
With right sides together carefully pin and baste the backing square to the canvaswork square. With the canvaswork uppermost, machine Straight Stitch around the edge of the stitchery. Leave a small opening. Trim away the excess fabric and carefully snip across the bulky fabric in the corners.

Turn the pin cushion to the right side and gently push a blunt pencil into each corner to help ease it into shape. Press if necessary and then stuff with some of the terylene or polyester filling. Fold in the raw edges of the opening and hand Slip Stitch the edges together to close.

Using matching thread, Slip Stitch the reserved twisted cord around the pin cushion, twisting it at each corner to form a small decorative loop. Finally, trim away the excess cord leaving both ends approximately 2.5 cm (1 in) long. Knot the ends before trimming them and then make fake tassels.

Iris Towel Border and Scented Sachet

This charming cross-stitch design of irises and stylized chrysanthemums is very versatile as not only does it make a beautiful border along a hand towel but it would also look stunning if applied to bed linen or table linen. The dainty hanging sachet could so easily become a pin cushion, or be made into the cover of a needle case.

The design is worked on Fine Aida fabric to give dense and rich areas of stitches in contrast to the plain unworked areas. It could be worked on a different gauge of fabric to make the design larger and bolder or smaller and finer. This particular fabric gives six Cross Stitches per cm (14 Cross Stitches per in).

As you are working from a charted design you could also interpret it into canvas-work; the smaller sachet design in particular would look extremely effective in Tent Stitch using tapisserie wool on canvas.

MATERIALS

(for the towel border)

Cream Fine Aida 14 count fabric, 20 × 70 cm (8 × 28 in) – any evenweave fabric of the same or similar gauge can be used but make allowances for a slight variation in scale
Cream hand towel, 56 cm (22 in) wide
Coat Anchor stranded thread: 1 skein each Blue 118, 940, Mauve 95, 98, Pink 74, 77, Yellow 305, Green 189, 208, 255
Cream sewing thread to match towel and fabric
Small rotating frame, or wooden embroidery hoop, 15 cm (6 in) diameter

Stitches used: *Cross Stitch, machine Satin Stitch, Slip Stitch.*

TO MAKE THE BORDER

1 If you are using a rotating frame mount the short ends of the Fine Aida fabric on the rotating sides of the frame and roll the excess fabric around one of these sides. If you are using a hoop place one end of the strip within the hoop. (You will find that you will have to reposition this several times as you work along the border. Similarly with the rotating frame you will have to adjust the position of the fabric by unrolling and rolling it around the rotating sides.)

2 Approximately 2.5 cm (1 in) in from the end of the strip of fabric find the centre of the width and mark it temporarily with a dressmaker's pin. This will help you position your cross-stitch border design centrally along the strip of fabric. Note that the centre of your border design is a line of stitches and not holes of the fabric.

3 Use two strands of thread at all times. Remember to work your Cross Stitches so that all the upper stitches face the same way for an even effect.

4 To begin the border start along the top black guideline and gradually work towards the bottom of the border chart. When you reach the bottom black guideline you will have completed one repeat section and are ready to repeat it again and again to give a continuous pattern. (The blue and yellow borders either side of the iris design are repeated over and over again as they do not fit exactly into the number of squares between the black triangles.)

You can choose which colour thread you wish to start with but remember to count outwards from the centre very carefully if you wish to begin your stitchery with either of the blue and yellow border patterns along the edges of the design.

The outer borders worked in blue and yellow threads can simply be repeated over and over again along the entire length of the towel strip, while the inner iris design is repeated every 63 stitches.

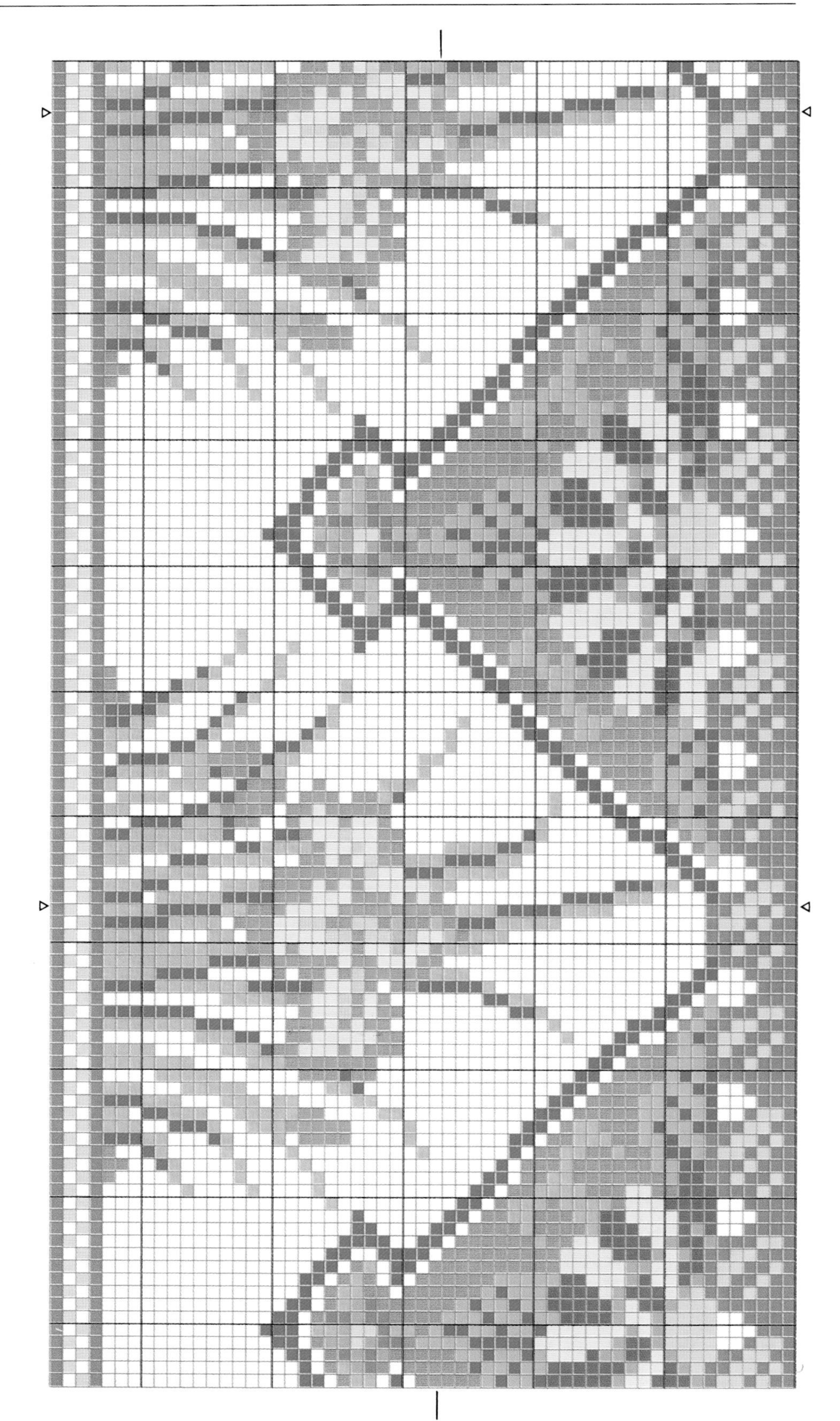

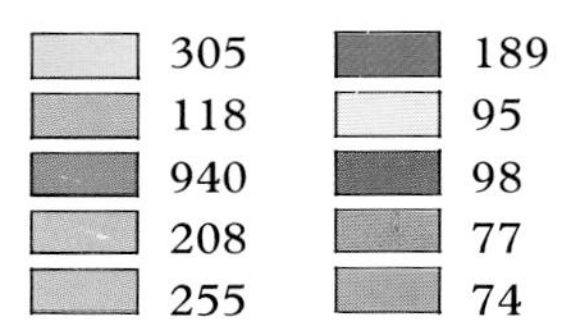

When you have worked the repeat section once or twice you will have become familiar with the way it is built up and fits together, but keep checking that your stitchery is accurate as it is very easy to count one too many or one too few stitches and thus distort the design quite drastically.

Continue repeating the design until you have worked approximately 60 cm (24 in). This length allows for the width of the towel plus a narrow turning at each end of the border. Adjust the length of the border if your towel is of a different size.

5 Remove the fabric from the frame or hoop and press it gently on the wrong side, using a stream iron. This will encourage the stitchery to stand out on the right side while flattening the fabric and removing any creases.

6 Trim away the surplus fabric along each side of the embroidered strip, leaving 6 mm (¼ in) allowance on either side (beyond the blue Cross Stitches). Similarly trim the surplus fabric at the short ends of the border, leaving 1 cm (⅜ in) at each end for a small turning.

7 Pin and baste the border across one end of the towel, tucking in the turned allowance at the short ends. If your towel has a woven brocade border, position the cross-stitch border so that it hides the woven pattern. Using cream sewing thread, machine Satin Stitch along the raw edges of the border, covering them completely with the width of the Satin Stitches and securely attaching the strip to the towel.

8 Finally, Slip Stitch the turned allowances to the towel sides to complete your Iris Towel border.

Scented Sachet

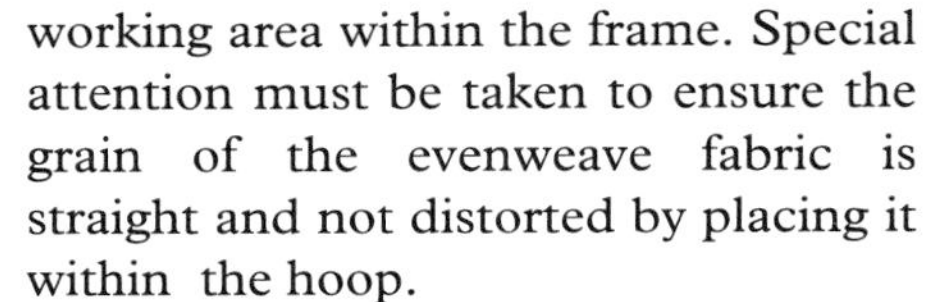

MATERIALS

Cream Fine Aida 14 count fabric, 25 cm (10 in) square

Cream lining fabric, 12.5 × 25 cm (5 × 10 in)

Coats Anchor stranded thread: 1 skein each Blue 118, 940, Mauve 95, 98, Pink 77, Yellow 305, Green 189, 208, 255

Coats Coton Perlé No. 5 thread: 1 skein each Blue 940, Yellow 305

Cream sewing thread

Blue or yellow sewing thread to match Coton Perlé thread

Cream fabric suitable to back sachet, 12.5 cm (5 in) square

Small amount of terylene or polyester filling

Small amount of pot pourri

Wooden embroidery hoop, 20 cm (8 in) diameter

TO MAKE THE SACHET

1 Place the Fine Aida fabric within the embroidery hoop and gently pull the edges of the fabric to create a taut working area within the frame. Special attention must be taken to ensure the grain of the evenweave fabric is straight and not distorted by placing it within the hoop.

2 Locate the position of the centre Cross Stitch within the working area of the hoop and commence your stitchery from this point, gradually working outwards. As with the towel border use two strands of thread at all times and ensure that all your stitches are even and face the same direction.

3 Once you have completed the cross-stitch design remove the fabric from the hoop and press it gently on the wrong side using a steam iron to encourage the stitches to stand out while removing any creases in the fabric.

4 Trim away the excess fabric leaving a 1 cm (⅜ in) seam allowance around the stitched design.

5 With right sides together pin and baste the stitched front and the cream backing piece of fabric together. Using cream sewing thread, machine Straight Stitch around the sachet working your seam line through the centre of the outside line of blue Cross Stitches. If worked carefully this will give an accurate diamond shape for the sachet. Leave a small opening.

Trim away the excess fabric across the corners of the seam allowance before turning the sachet to the right side. Carefully push out the corner points and smooth the sachet into shape.

Measure the size of the sachet and then make a lining bag of the same size using the lining fabric. Leave a small opening to match that of the sachet cover.

Carefully push the lining bag inside the sachet so that their openings coincide with each other. Fill with a mixture of stuffing material and pot pourri. Tuck in the open edges of the lining bag and hand Slip Stitch the edges together to close. Repeat with the open edges of the sachet.

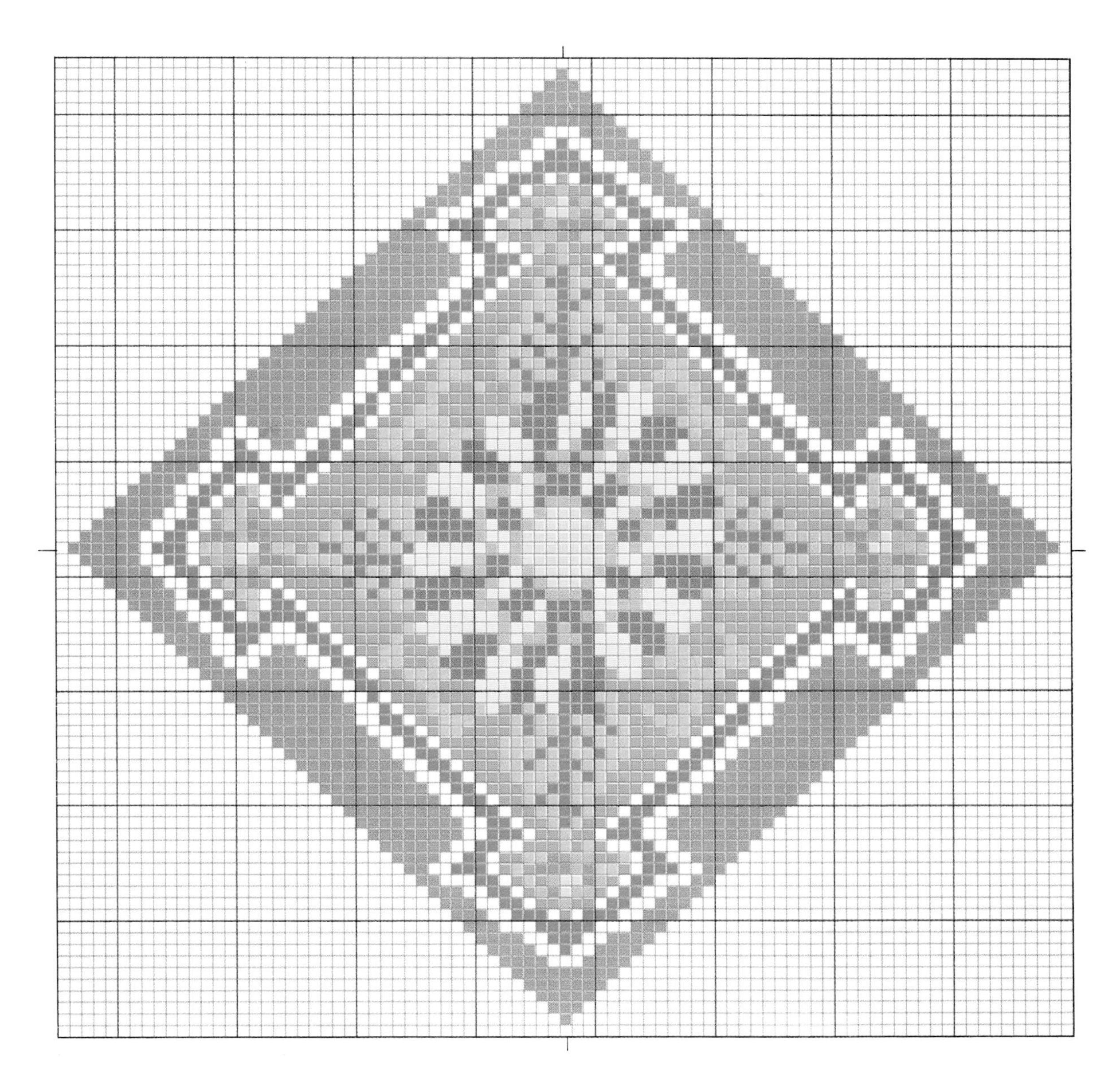

6 Make a length of two-colour twisted cord using the blue and yellow Coton Perlé thread. Cut six lengths of each colour, each length measuring 1 m (1⅛ yd) (see Special Techniques page 138).
7 Pin the cord around the sachet arranging it to leave an extra 12.5 cm (5 in) at one corner. Make this into a loop and then allow both ends of the cord to hang loose at the corner opposite the loop.

Using either blue or yellow sewing thread, Slip Stitch the cord securely around the sachet.

Arrange the loose ends of the cord into a false bow and sew it securely in position (if you try to tie a real bow you will find it is too bulky and unattractive).

Trim the ends of the cord, knotting them and teasing out the ends into mock tassels to complete your Scented Sachet.

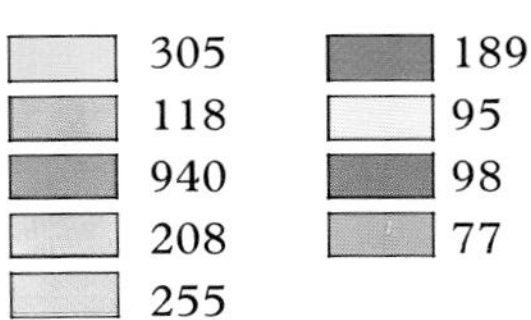

Strutting Crane Sachet

These unusual scented sachets will gently perfume the area in which they are hung. I was inspired to make them by a small hexagonal porcelain lid which displays motifs of cranes and quails and simple sprays of flowers and foliage. The cranes are used as symbols of longevity and the quails symbolize courage.

I have used the two strutting cranes and some of the foliage to make two motifs, one for each side of the first scented sachet. Then by reversing the motifs and working them as mirror images I made a second sachet.

The sachets are decoratively hung by a green, silky loop with four elegant leaves to give an appearance of a hanging fruit.

MATERIALS

(for one sachet)

White silky-type fabric, 25 × 50 cm (10 × 20 in)
White cotton backing fabric, 25 × 50 cm (10 × 20 in)
Emerald-green silky-type fabric, 30 × 40 cm (12 × 16 in)
Coats Anchor stranded embroidery thread: 1 skein each Grey 231, 236, Blue 117, 118, Rust 337, 339, Green 186, 204, 206
Sewing thread, white, and to match green silky fabric
Small amount of terylene or polyester filling
Small amount of pot pourri
Double knitting or tapestry wool, any colour
Blue-coloured crayon
Embroidery hoop, 20 cm (8 in) diameter
Fine-tipped black felt pen
Tracing paper

Stitches used: *Back Stitch, Fly Stitch, Satin Stitch, Encroaching Straight Stitch, French Knots, Fishbone Stitch, Seeding Stitch, Basting Stitch, machine Straight Stitch, Top Stitch, Slip Stitch.*

TO MAKE THE SACHET

1 Accurately trace the two motifs on to tracing paper using the felt pen.

2 Press the white fabrics to remove any creases. Fold each piece in half and cut along the fold line to give two pieces of each fabric, all measuring 25 cm (10 in) square.

3 Stretch one piece of silky fabric within the hoop and lay it over the trace-off pattern so that the fabric is resting on the tracing paper. (If you place the trace-off pattern on a white surface you will see the design lines very clearly through the fine silky fabric.) Using the blue crayon trace all the design lines centrally on to the fabric. Do not trace the seam line. Ensure the crayon is kept sharpened.

Repeat this process with the remaining square of silky fabric and the second crane motif.

4 Place one of your prepared silky squares on top of one of the backing squares and then mount them within the embroidery hoop, gently pulling the fabric around the outside edges of the hoop until the layers of fabric are smooth and taut within the hoop.

5 It does not matter which motif you work to begin with. They are both worked in a very similar way. If you have two hoops of the correct size you can work the two motifs simultaneously.

Use two strands of embroidery thread at all times. To work the cranes use dark Grey to give the outline shapes, working tiny, evenly-sized Back Stitches along the gently curved design lines of the body, along each edge of the beak, and along the very thin legs and feet. The scalloped edges of the wings and tail are worked in Fly Stitches (see page 110). You will find it best to work these stitches after the

Trace-off patterns and colour guides for the sachets.

bird has been filled in with solid stitchery. Also, the rows of Back Stitches that are on the underside of the flapping wings are more pronounced if worked once the wings have been filled in.

The beak is filled in with Satin Stitch worked horizontally across the width of the beak which you have already outlined in Back Stitches. By working over and across these Back Stitches you will achieve a rich and slightly raised effect.

The light Grey body of each crane is filled with small Straight Stitches that are worked directionally from the head down to the tail to give a feeling of plumage. The small stitches are worked quite freely and are called Encroaching Straight Stitches. As the name suggests, they encroach upon one another giving a sketched or drawn effect (see page 82). The blue wings are also worked in this way with the stitches being worked from the top edge down towards the tip of each wing.

Once all the solid areas of the crane are filled then complete the bird with a single French Knot for the eye and the Fly Stitches on the wings and tail, as mentioned earlier. The crane with the flapping wings is completed by emphasizing the scalloped Fly Stitch edging up into the wing by working neat lines of Back Stitches.

The foliage of each motif is worked quite simply. Fishbone Stitches are employed for the leaves, using three shades of green for the leaves of the flapping crane while the two deeper shades of green are used for the leaves of the other crane motif. The stems are worked in small green Back Stitches varying the shade of green according to the shade of the leaves near to it. The stems are thickened by working broken lines of Back Stitches. Use the lighter shade of rust for the stems of the flapping crane motif and the darker shade of rust for the stems of the other motif.

Then work the seed pods in light and dark Rust French Knots using the lighter shade for the pointed tip of the pods and changing to the darker shade towards the rounded base of the pods.

Finally, work the ground areas of the motifs. The flapping crane stands on a ground area of lots of tiny, randomly-spaced French Knots. Use dark Grey, gradually changing to dark Rust and then to light Rust. The other crane stands on a ground area of light Green Seeding Stitches with wavy lines of dark Rust Back Stitches worked over the Seeding Stitches.

6 When you have completed the embroidery accurately cut around the dotted seam line of the paper pattern and place this over the embroidered motif. Baste around the edges of the

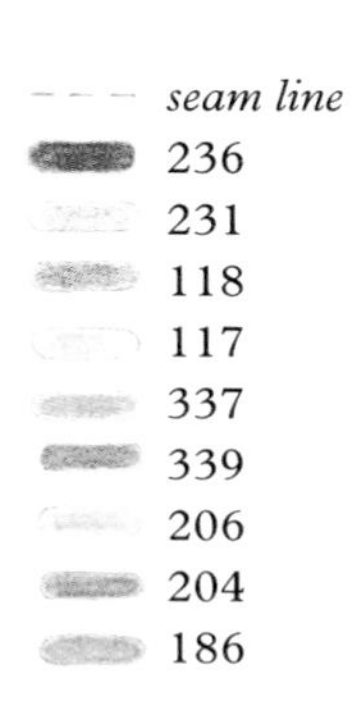

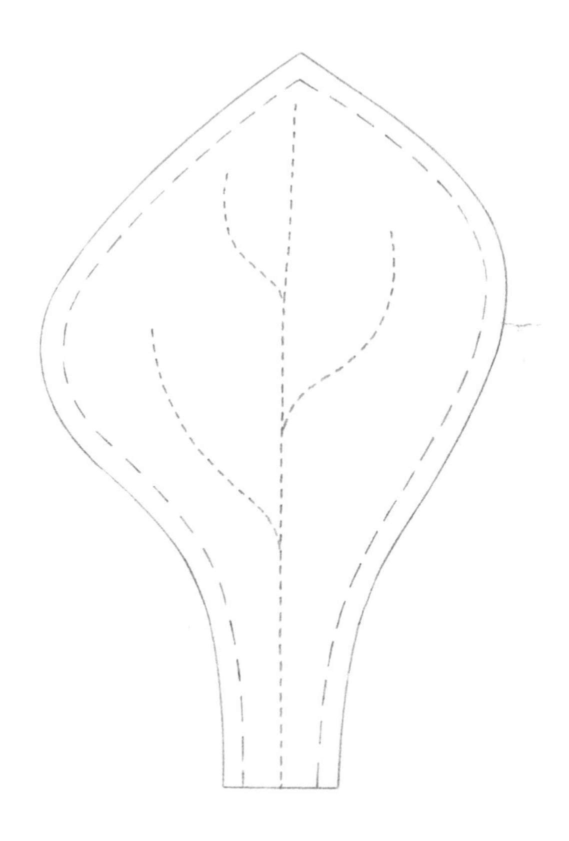

paper shape to give your seam line on the fabric layers. Repeat this around the other motif.

7 Remove the fabric from the hoop and trim away the excess fabric leaving a 1 cm (⅜ in) seam allowance. Repeat for the second motif.

8 With right sides together pin and baste the two shapes together. Using white sewing thread machine Straight Stitch around the curved edge of the sachet shape.

The small straight edge across the top of the sachet is left unstitched but this is not large enough to turn the shape inside out through, so do not stitch right up to this but allow for a bigger opening. Clip the seam allowance in towards the line of machine stitching around the curved shape.

Turn each sachet to the right side easing it into shape. Fill softly with a mixture of pot pourri and your chosen filling. Do not overfill as your aim is to achieve a flattish, soft object.

9 Make the leaves and loop.

Trace and cut out the leaf shape (see

Top, Trace-off pattern for the leaves. The solid line is the cutting line; the strong dotted line is the seam line; and the fine dotted line is the suggested top stitching line.

Right, Fly Stitch. Use this stitch to give scalloped edges to the wing and tail feathers of the cranes.

Opposite, Using Basting Stitch, arrange the four leaves and hanging loop in place then sew firmly together.

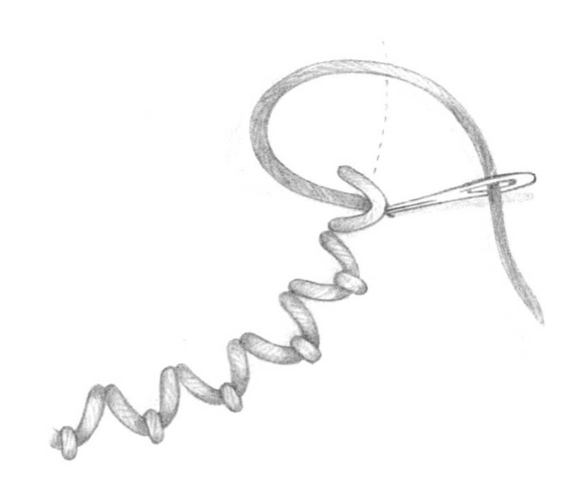

opposite) and use it as a template to cut out eight shapes from the green silky fabric. Then cut out a long, thin strip measuring 1.5×40 cm (⅝×16 in).

Pin and baste the leaf shapes together in pairs to make four leaves. Then, with matching thread, machine Straight Stitch around the shapes leaving the small straight edges open. Snip the seam allowance in towards the line of stitching and clip across the point of the seam allowance. Then turn each leaf to the right side and ease into shape. Top Stitch the central and lateral veins of each leaf as suggested on the trace-off pattern.

With right sides together, fold the long, thin strip in half and machine Straight Stitch along the length of the strip allowing a very narrow seam. Using a small safety pin turn the long strip to the right side (see Lucky Bats page 98 for this technique). Thread a few lengths of wool through the channel of the thin strip to fill it softly.

Fold the strip in half placing the raw ends together and baste to hold. Then arrange the four leaves around the raw ends of the loop and baste their stems to hold them in position (see right). At this stage you can shorten the loop if desired.

10 Push the raw ends of the leaves and loop inside the small opening of the sachet. Turn in the open edges of the white silky fabric to follow the curved line of the side seam and then straight across the short top edge. With a double length of sewing thread carefully and securely Slip Stitch the side seam closed and then across the top straight edge, at the same time firmly stitching the leaves and loop in place. This completes your hanging scented sachets.

Spotted Deer Greetings Cards

These charming cross-stitch cards can be made with only a small amount of materials and can be quickly completed. You can experiment with the scale of the design and use larger or smaller blank cards to mount your work within. You can also use these simple designs to make wall pictures, small pin cushions or scented sachets.

MATERIALS

(for each card)

Purchased greetings card, white, 12.5 × 18 cm (5 × 7¼ in) with an oval window measuring 9 × 13.5 cm (3½ × 5¼ in)

White Fine Aida 14 count fabric, 25 cm (10 in) square

Small amounts of Coats Anchor stranded embroidery thread: Blue 120, 132, 136, Rust 339, 880

Clear adhesive glue suitable for fabric and card

Wooden embroidery hoop, 20 cm (8 in) diameter

(Optional twisted cord made from Coats Coton Perlé No. 5 Rust 340, Blue 131)

Stitches used: *Cross Stitch.*

TO MAKE THE GREETINGS CARD

1 Place the fabric in the hoop, making sure the grain is straight.

2 Following one of the charts overleaf, work the deer motif and the surrounding blue background shapes using the centre guidelines to help you find and commence stitching in the middle of the fabric.

Use three strands of thread at all times. Each Cross Stitch is worked over one horizontal and vertical set of threads.

Ensure that all your Cross Stitches are worked in the same way so that they give a uniform appearance. It does not really matter which way your uppermost stitches are facing as long as they all face the same way.

3 Once your design is complete remove the fabric from the hoop. Press the wrong side of the fabric gently with a steam iron to give the stitchery an embossed effect.

4 Open the card out flat and place the window section of it over the deer motif. Estimate how much fabric has to be cut away then trim the surplus so that the design fits within the frame but allows a deep enough border to overlap the frame and be glued to the card.

5 Use the clear glue to hold the design centrally within the window and then fold the backing section over the wrong side of the design and glue them together to complete the greetings card.

NB: If your greetings card does not have quite the same-sized window you may have to add more of the randomly-scattered Cross Stitches to fill the background area effectively.

If you find it difficult to purchase the ready-made cards you can make your own quite easily (see Special Techniques page 139).

6 To complete your greetings card make a two-colour twisted cord using three lengths of Blue and three of Rust Coton Perlé thread, each length measuring 75 cm (30 in), (see Special Techniques page 138). Tie the cord around the card at its fold so that the knot lies at the base. Tease out the cut loose ends of the cord to make fake tassels then trim them for a neat finish.

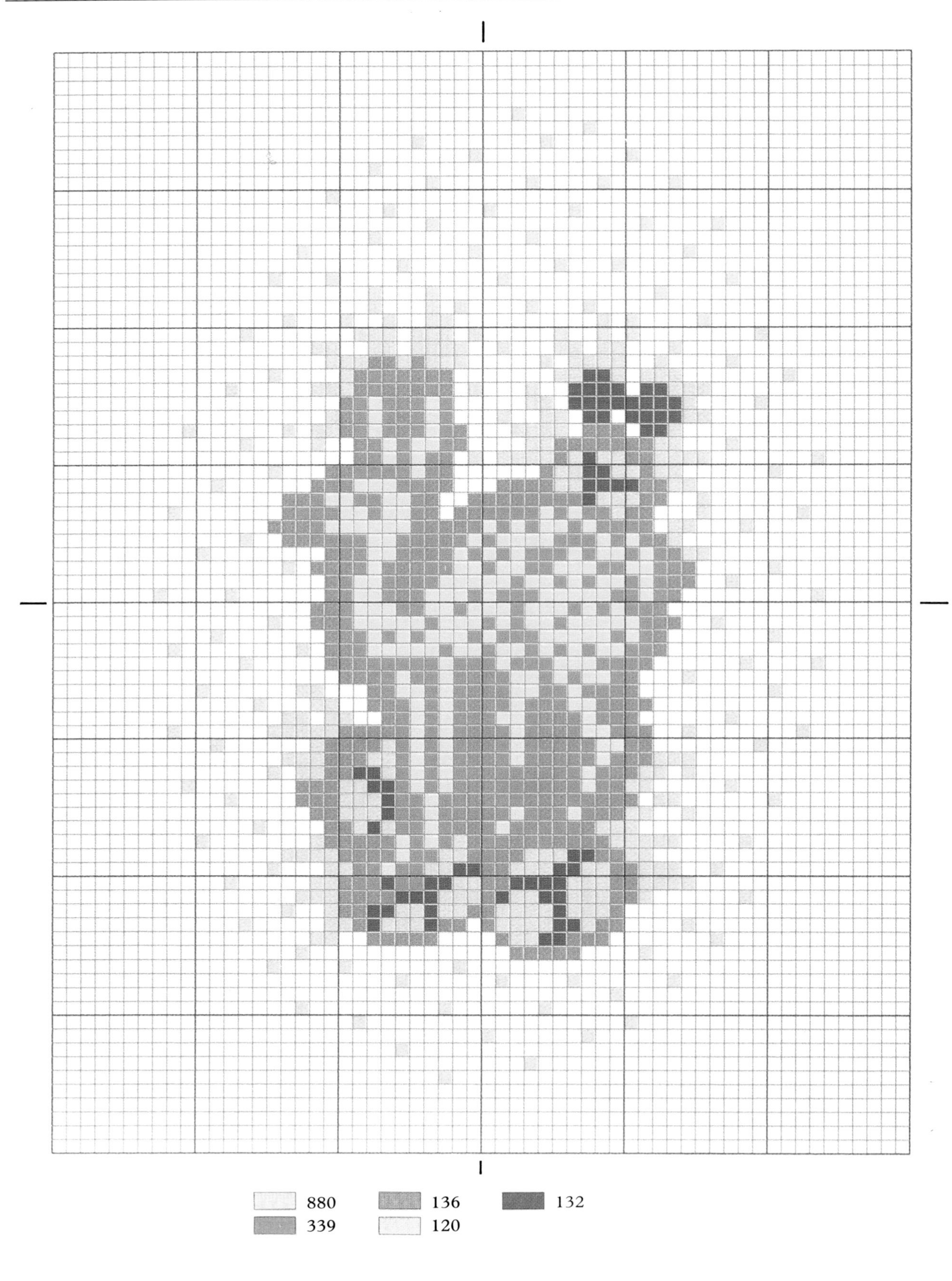
880
136
132
339
120

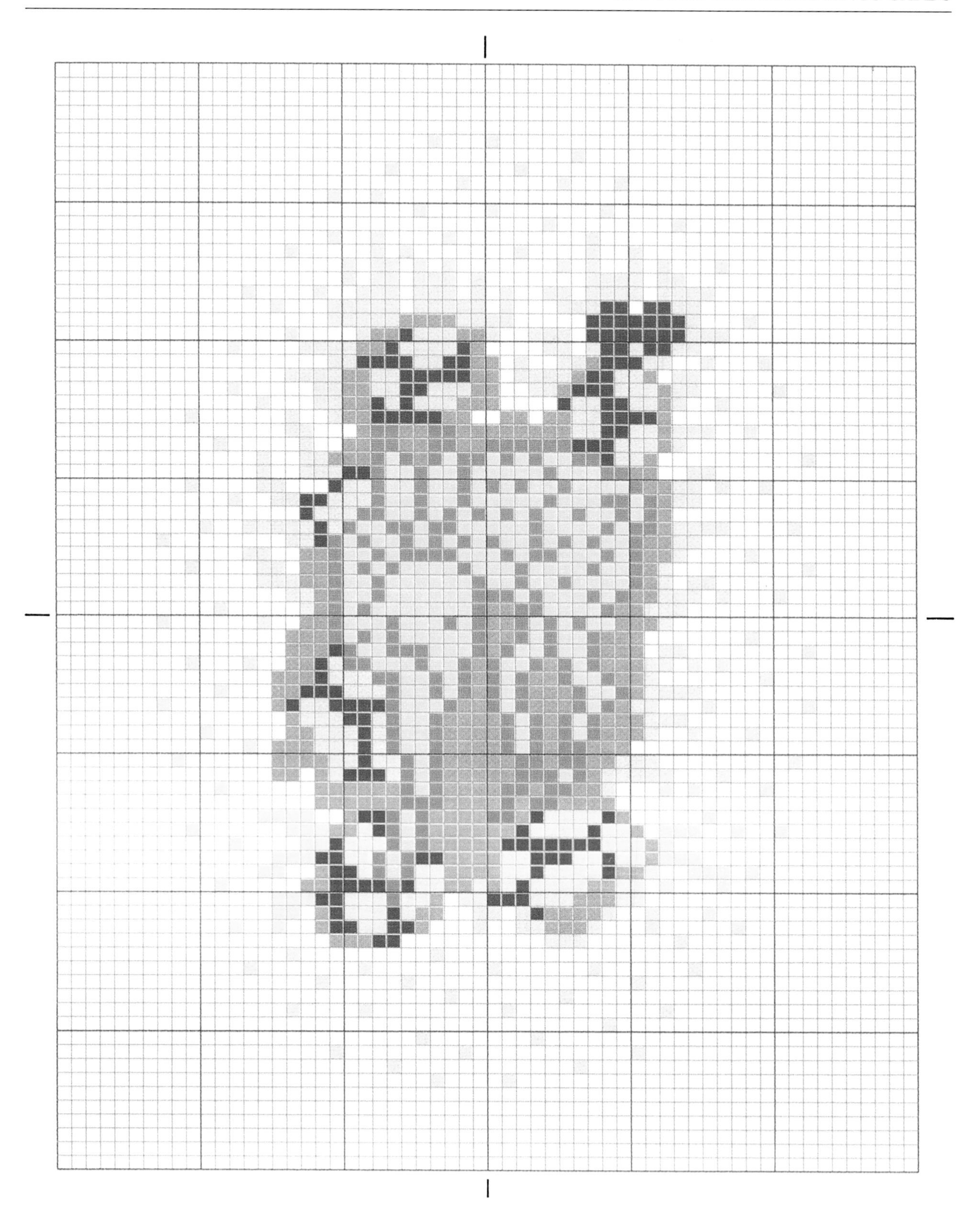

Pair of Patchwork Pillows

The rich colours and the variety of techniques and materials used to produce these small scented pillows add a jewel-like quality to each of them. Inspired by a large porcelain dish in the Victoria & Albert Museum, London, I have selected two main themes from the dish: the fish swimming around the design; contrasted with the geometric patterns achieved by the central patchwork sections. One of these sections is of simple hexagonal patchwork; the other is the more complicated cathedral window patchwork.

The pillows require patience and some practised skill but are a delight to reproduce and worth all the effort. Each is worked in sections which are finally brought together to give rich and glowing results.

Peach Cathedral Patchwork Pillow

MATERIALS

Pale-peach cotton lawn fabric, two pieces – 38 cm (15 in) square and 23 cm (9 in) square
White cotton backing fabric, two pieces – 38 cm (15 in) square and 23 cm (9 in) square
Strips of jade-green cotton fabric (cut on the bias) or Bias binding, 2.5 cm (1 in) wide when opened flat and 90 cm (36 in) long
Magenta-purple satin ribbon, 3 mm (1/8 in) wide and 1 m (1 1/8 yd) long
Dark-rose satin ribbon, 3 mm (1/8 in) wide and 1 m (1 1/8 yd) long
Jade-green cotton lawn fabric to match the bias strip, 30 cm (12 in) square
Small amounts of rusty-red, dark-rose and peach cotton lawn fabric
Coats Anchor stranded embroidery thread: 1 skein each Purple 92, 972, Blue 118, Green 185, 189, 206, 230, Beige 276, 367
Sewing threads to match the satin ribbons and the pale peach and jade-green fabrics
Double knitting or tapestry wool, any colour, to pipe the binding strip
A little pot pourri
Polyester or terylene filling
Coloured crayon
Fine-tipped black felt pen
Tracing paper
Small piece of thin card
Embroidery frame, 30 cm (12 in) square
Masking tape

Stitches used: *Satin Stitch, Buttonhole Stitch, Back Stitch, Fly Stitch, French Knot, Couching Stitch, Stab Stitch, Basting Stitch, Oversewing or Whip Stitch, Single Chain Stitch, machine Straight Stitch, Slip Stitch.*

TO MAKE THE PEACH PILLOW

1 Press all the fabrics and ribbons to remove any creases.

Stretch the larger square of backing fabric over the frame, ensuring the grain of the fabric lies parallel with the sides of the frame.

Trace the pillow design on page 118 on to tracing paper then fix this temporarily to a clean, flat surface (preferably white). Place the larger square of peach lawn centrally over the tracing. Gently smooth and tape the fabric in position and, using a sharp-pointed coloured crayon, accurately trace the four corner motifs of fish and shells on to the fabric. Do not trace the dotted seam line or the ribbon lines. Release the fabric and the trace-off pattern. Reserve the traced pattern.

Stretch the fabric over the frame, ensuring the grain is straight.

2 You are now ready to work the embroidery in each corner of the pillow. Use two strands of embroidery thread at all times unless otherwise stated.

Follow the colour guide (see page 118) of the fish and shell motif and refer to the picture below to help you. Each fish is worked in Satin Stitches placing the stitches across the width of the various shapes and spacing them evenly and closely side by side to one another.

Close-up detail of the corner. See overleaf for the trace-off pattern.

The spiral shell shape at the side of the fish head is made in neat Buttonhole Stitches, working them so that the bars of the stitches lie on the outer edges of the spiral shape then, as the shape diminishes into a line, change your stitches into tiny Back Stitches worked around the mouth of the fish.

The eye is worked in Buttonhole Stitches, again with the bars laying on the outer edge of the circular shape. Highlight the eye with a French Knot.

Work the decorative scale pattern on top of the Satin Stitch body area in a very effective variation of Fly Stitch (see Fish and Waterlily Bath Linen, page 43).

The two small green shells are worked in spirals of Buttonhole Stitches working from the centre outwards.

The larger sea urchin shells are worked in Couching Stitches. Six strands of the thread are held in position by only two strands across them. Work these from the centres outwards, gently curving the thicker thread and laying it down quite loosely to produce the slightly raised effect.

3 Cut each of the dark-rose and magenta-purple satin ribbons into four pieces of equal length (eight pieces in all). Then lay them on the stretched fabric arranging them and overlapping them where they intersect one another

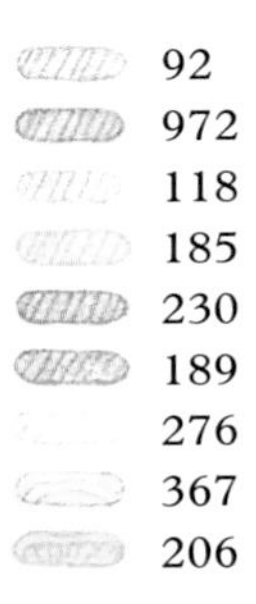

as indicated on the trace-off pattern.

You may find it useful to place the trace-off pattern over the stretched fabric and slip the ribbons under the paper adjusting their position as necessary. Carefully pin them to hold. Then, using matching sewing thread, work tiny Stab Stitches along each side of each length of ribbon.

4 Make the cathedral window patchwork section. The technique of cathedral window patchwork is a particularly effective method of folding and stitching small pieces of fabric together. It demands accuracy in cutting and measuring but it is well worth the extra care required.

Accurately cut out nine jade-green squares each measuring 9 cm (3½ in). Ensure that the sides of the squares lay on the straight grain of the fabric. You can make a template to help you if you wish (see page 120).

Make the smaller template using a scrap of thin card or firm paper and use this to help you fold the turning allowance of each green patch. Finger press the folded edges around the template shape, carefully tucking in the extra layers of fabric at each corner. Remove the template and then baste the folded edges to hold in place.

With the turned edges facing you, fold the corners to meet at the centre point. Baste to hold at the centre. Then fold the new corners to meet

Opposite, Colour trace-off pattern and stitch guide for one quarter of the design. Make a tracing of this section and repeat it three more times to form a complete design. The quarter trace-off is shown full size, and you do not need to trace the central cathedral window section. Your final drawing should look like an enlarged version of the position guide (left). When you then transfer the traced design on to the fabric only transfer the fish and shell motifs (not the ribbon position guides).

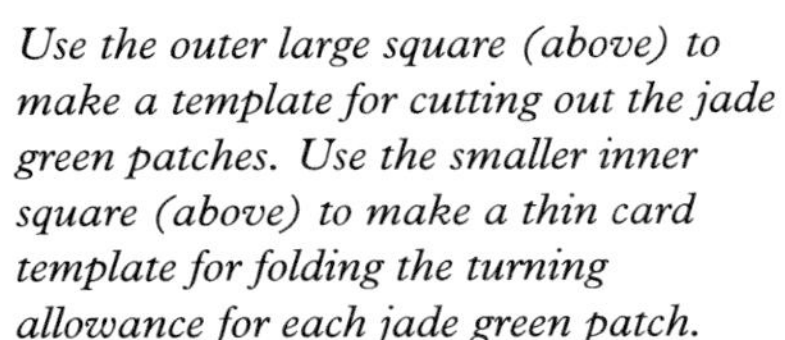

Use the outer large square (above) to make a template for cutting out the jade green patches. Use the smaller inner square (above) to make a thin card template for folding the turning allowance for each jade green patch.

Left, Use this tiny square to make a template to help you cut out the small patches.

each other at the centre and once more baste to hold. Accurately repeat this process of folding and basting with each of the remaining fabric squares.

5 From the small pieces of rusty-red, dark-rose and peach fabrics accurately cut out your small squares to fill the cathedral windows. Make sure the edges of each square correspond with the straight grain of the fabric. You will need four rusty-red squares, eight dark-rose squares and twelve peach squares, each measuring 2 cm (¾ in) square. You can make a template if you wish (see left).

Then, with the folded sides of the prepared jade-green squares facing towards each other and using matching sewing thread, sew the squares together in three rows of three squares to produce a larger square. Use small Oversewing or Whip Stitches to catch the edges of the squares joining them all together.

Press gently on the wrong side.

6 Place the four rusty-red squares over the central jade squares that have been formed (each has a seam line diagonally through it) and pin to hold, then arrange the eight dark-rose squares around them, and finally place the twelve peach squares around the edges (these will hang over the edges of the jade shape).

Turn back the folded jade-green edges over the raw edges of the smaller squares. As you do this you will find that the folded edges will curve gently because they lie on the bias of the fabric. Stitch these curved edges with matching thread through all the layers to hold the contrasting squares in place.

The inner rusty-red and dark-rose squares can be stitched on all sides but the outer peach squares can only be stitched on two sides. Fold under the overlap to the wrong side of the patchwork piece and stitch to hold (see opposite above). Your panel of cathedral window patchwork is now complete.

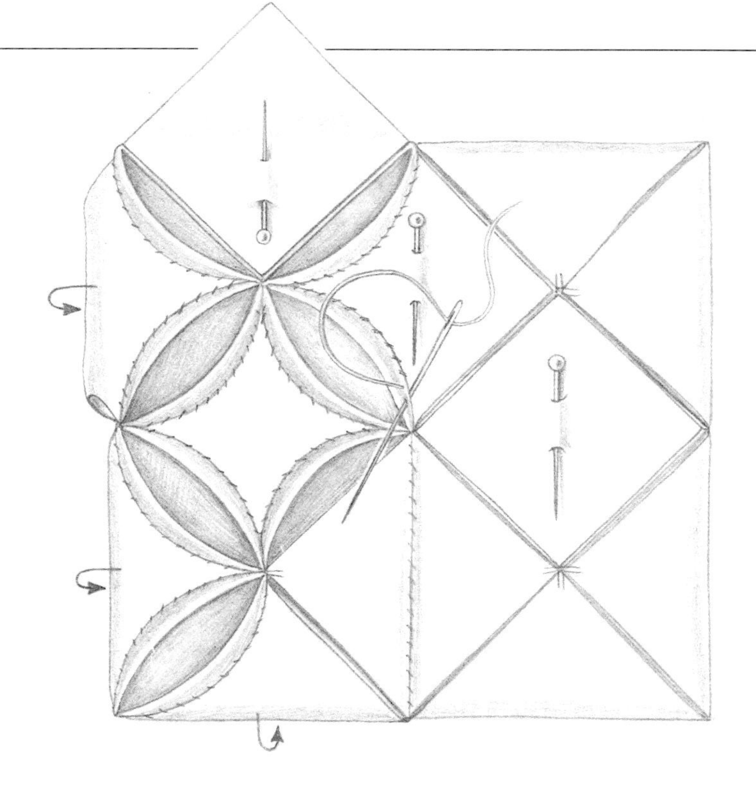

Making the cathedral window patchwork centre panel. Opposite below, Sew all the prepared jade green squares together to form a large square. Left, Fold the outer square patches that hang over the panel to the wrong side and stitch to hold them in position. See the photograph below for a detailed view.

7 Pin the panel centrally within the square formed by the arrangement of satin ribbons on the frame and, using matching thread, carefully and invisibly hand-sew it in position using small Stab Stitches. (Use the trace-off pattern to place the panel accurately on the fabric frame.)

Following the colour plan, work a stylized flower in each of the curved diamond shapes within the patchwork. Each flower is formed by working a central French Knot with four Single Chain Stitches around the knot. Work only three Single Chain Stitches around the knots on the peachy shapes as these are incomplete.

8 Trim the trace-off pattern along the dotted seam line, and aligning the design areas, pin the pattern to the embroidered fabric. Baste around the cut paper edge. Remove the fabric layers from the frame and trim away the surplus fabric leaving a 1 cm ($^{3}/_{8}$ in) seam allowance around the basted seam line.

9 Make the piping edge for the pillow as follows.

If you are making your own bias strip for the piping edge, cut several 2.5 cm (1 in) wide strips on the bias of the jade-green fabric. Join the strips diagonally so that they produce one continuous length measuring 90 cm (36 in) long. Fold this strip in half lengthwise. If using purchased bias binding, press the strip open and flat, then fold it in half lengthwise.

Machine stitch along the bias strip to produce a narrow seam or channel 5 mm ($^{3}/_{16}$ in) wide. Thread several lengths of double knitting or tapestry wool through the channel, using a large tapestry needle or bodkin to give a gently rounded piped edging.

Pin and baste the piped edging along the basted seam line of the pillow face. Then very carefully machine stitch the piping in position (begin and end the piping at one corner).

With right sides together, place the small square of peach fabric over the embroidered square, then place the small white backing square on top of the plain peach square. Smooth all the layers together matching up their edges.

Pin, baste and then machine Straight Stitch the layers together, working with the embroidered layers facing you so that you can follow the line of stitching that you worked when adding the piped edging. Leave a small opening.

Clip the excess fabric across the corners and trim the layers of fabric around the seam line. Turn the pillow to the right side. Stuff gently with a mixture of pot pourri and the terylene or polyester filling. Tuck in the open edges and Slip Stitch them together along the seam line to complete the pillow.

BLUE HEXAGONAL PATCHWORK PILLOW

MATERIALS

Pale royal-blue cotton lawn fabric, two pieces – 38 cm (15 in) square and 23 cm (9 in) square

White cotton backing fabric, two pieces – 38 cm (15 in) square and 23 cm (9 in) square

Strip of rusty-red cotton fabric (cut on the bias) or bias binding, 2.5 cm (1 in) wide when opened flat and 90 cm (36 in) long

Dark jade-green satin ribbon, 7 mm (5/16 in) wide and 1 m (1 1/8 yd) long

Forest-green satin ribbon, 2 mm (1/16 in) wide and 1 m (1 1/8 yd) long

Rusty-red cotton lawn fabric to match the bias strip, 16 cm (6 1/4 in) square

Small amounts of jade-green, light green, turquoise and light royal-blue cotton lawn fabrics

Coats Anchor stranded embroidery thread: 1 skein each Purple 92, 972, Blue 118, 178, Green 185, 189, 206, 230, Beige 276, 367, Rust 337, 339, 341
Sewing threads to match the satin ribbons, the rusty-red and pale royal-blue fabrics
Double knitting or tapestry wool, any colour, to pipe the binding strip
A little pot pourri
Polyester or terylene wadding
Coloured crayon
Fine-tipped black felt pen
Plain paper
Tracing paper
Small piece of thin card
Embroidery frame, 30 cm (12 in) square
Masking tape

Stitches used: *Satin Stitch, Buttonhole Stitch, Back Stitch, Fly Stitch, Couching Stitch, machine Straight Stitch, Basting Stitch, Oversewing or Whip Stitch, Stab Stitch, French Knots, Single Chain Stitch.*

TO MAKE THE BLUE PILLOW

1 Follow step 1 (page 117) for the peach pillow, substituting the peach fabric with blue, and the magenta and rose satin ribbons with the green shades and using the trace-off pattern.
2 Work the embroidery of the fishes and shells in each corner, once more following the instructions for the peach pillow (see step 2, pages 117-18) and using the colour plan/trace-off pattern below to guide you with the different shades of thread.
3 Using the appropriate coloured satin ribbons follow step 3 (pages 118-19) of the peach pillow to stitch them in position around the outside of the embroidered corner motifs.
4 Make the hexagonal patchwork

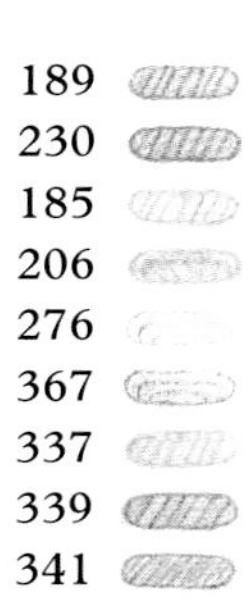

Opposite, Colour trace-off pattern and stitch guide for one quarter of the design. Make a tracing of this section and repeat it three more times to form a complete design. The quarter trace-off is shown full size. The dotted line is a position guideline for the central patchwork section. Your final drawing should look like an enlarged version of the position guide (left). When you then transfer the traced design on to the fabric only transfer the fish and shell motifs.

centre section. Hexagonal patchwork is much more simple and straightforward than cathedral window patchwork but it still requires accuracy both in cutting out the templates and stitching the patches together. Ideally, each fabric shape should be positioned and cut out so that two opposite edges of the hexagon shape lie parallel with the straight grain of the fabric and then when the patches are sewn together they are arranged so that the straight grain of all the patches lies in the same direction. This prevents the pieces stretching against one another.

Very accurately trace and cut out of thin card or firm paper the small hexagonal template (see page 126). Then in turn use this template to cut out thirty-one paper hexagons which you will cover temporarily with the fabric patches.

5 Cut out the fabric patches. To do this hold the card template over the fabric and cut around the shape adding a small turning allowance all round of approximately 6 mm (¼ in).

Cut out six jade-green shapes, eight light-green shapes, nine turquoise shapes and eight light royal-blue shapes. Carefully cover your paper shapes with the slightly larger fabric shapes, folding the turning allowance around the edge of the paper and basting to hold it in place to produce an accurate fabric hexagon.

6 With blue sewing thread and right sides together, stitch the patches to each other using tiny Oversewing or Whip Stitches and following the

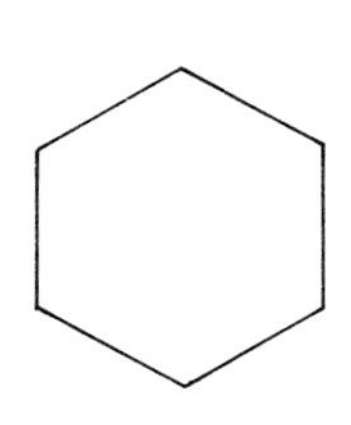

Above, Hexagon template, full size. Accurately trace and cut out this small hexagon shape to be used as the template when preparing your patches.

Right, Colour plan and stitch guide for the central patchwork panel. Follow this arrangement when stitching your tiny hexagon patches together. When you have mounted them within the rusty-red shape, follow this guide to embroider the stylized flowers. You will find it helpful also to refer to the photograph opposite.

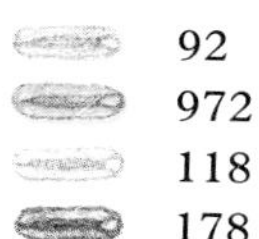

92
972
118
178

colour plan above. Remember to align the straight grain of all the patches (see step 4 on page 125). Once you have stitched all the small patches together remove all the basting threads so that each of the tiny paper hexagons can be released. If your oversewing stitches are very neat and small then you will find that the papers will fall away easily.

7 Prepare the rusty-red shape as follows. Fold a 1 cm (3/8 in) turning to the wrong side along each edge of the rusty-red square, carefully folding the corners and tucking in the excess fabric. Baste to hold in position.

Fold in the corner points to meet each other at the centre of the square with the right side on the outside. Finger-press the new shape and then baste the folded corners at the centre to hold them firmly in place.

Press the piece of patchwork gently on the wrong side to flatten and smooth it.

Place the patchwork on top of the folded side of the rusty-red square. The centre turquoise patch needs to lie over the centre point of the square; pin to hold in position.

Trim the patchwork so that it is slightly smaller (approximately 3 mm

(⅛ in)) than the square. Gently fold the edges of the square over and around the cut raw edges of the patchwork. You will find that because they lie on the bias of the fabric they will curve into neat arcs. Using matching sewing thread, sew along the curved edges with tiny Stab Stitches to hold the rusty-red fabric over the patchwork.

You will notice that the finished shape echoes that of the cathedral window patchwork.

8 Pin the patchwork shape centrally within the blank space between the embroidered fish. Then, with matching thread, carefully sew it in position working tiny invisible Stab Stitches along the curved edges of the rusty-red fabric and through the stretched blue background fabric.

Finally, work a tiny stylized flower in the centre of each hexagon patch (see the colour guide opposite). The centre of each flower is a small French Knot and around this work Single Chain Stitches. Where the patches are not complete then work only part of a flower (see detail).

9 Make up the pillow by following the instructions for making up the peach pillow (see steps 8 and 9 page 122), using the rusty-red bias strips to make the piped edging, and the blue backing fabric.

Although the techniques used to make each pillow are different, the final results complement each other beautifully.

Special Techniques

One of the joys of embroidery is that there is not a great deal of equipment needed to produce a beautiful piece of work. Also, it is possible to begin embroidery with a limited number of items and then, as your interest grows, you can gradually add to your equipment and stocks of fabric and yarn.

For example, you may begin with one or two embroidery hoops and then collect more of different sizes, as well as rectangular frames.

Always take care of the equipment that you use for your embroidery, especially scissors which become blunt very quickly if they are used to cut paper. It is always tempting to cut paper with sharp trimming scissors if they are close to hand, but do not give in as paper-cutting really does spoil them for cutting fabric.

It is important to keep everything very clean and damp-free; a dusty embroidery hoop will leave a mark on any fabric that is placed in it, possibly spoiling many hours of work. Similarly, a rusty needle or pin will mark, damage or ruin a piece of work. So store everything very carefully and discard anything that may spoil your work.

Your sewing basket should include a good selection of basic sewing items, such as a variety of crewel and tapestry needles as well as ordinary sewing needles, fine crochet hooks, scissors labelled to remind you of their uses, thimbles, marking pencils of different colours, etc., plus all your own personally gathered favourites that you find so useful.

Fabrics

Try to collect a good selection of fabrics. You will notice that many of the projects in this book call for relatively simple, inexpensive fabrics such as cotton or cotton polyester; those fabrics which are more costly are used economically so that none of the projects is too expensive, and you will find that all can be used in a variety of ways. You will find it useful to keep even the narrow strips cut away from around your finished embroidery and use them when trying out stitches or masking pencils, etc.

Always back your fabric where it is recommended in the instructions, as the extra layer (usually of a similar weight to the top fabric) will give more body to the top layer, strengthening it and making handling easier.

However, remember that you must baste the two layers together carefully with diagonal basting stitches (see page 137) if the embroidery is to be worked freely in the hand or in a hoop. If it is to be worked on a frame, you need not baste the layers together (unless instructed to do so) as the fabrics are mounted layer by layer on the frame.

If the fabric you are using is very soft and flimsy, you can use spray starch on the wrong side to stiffen it slightly, ready for working. Spray starch can also be used on the finished stitchery if you want a very crisp, fresh, well-laundered look.

Always test spray starch on a spare piece of fabric to ensure it is suitable, as it may leave spots on some fabrics.

Threads and Yarns

With the growing popularity of needlecrafts and embroidery, there is a similar growth in the availability of all the various threads and yarns that are recommended.

Most of the threads are made of cotton or wool, and the range of colours is extensive and steadily growing.

Always consider the type of thread in relation to the effect you wish to achieve. Some threads can be divided, giving a very fine and delicate effect or a thicker one; others cannot be split, as their fibres are twisted together when they are being spun. Also there is a difference between matt, hairy woollen yarns and the lustrous, shiny effect of cotton yarns. If you are in doubt about the effect you wish to achieve, make a few test stitches on a spare piece of fabric.

The following threads are used in this book:

Stranded thread (sometimes known as embroidery floss) is a slightly lustrous thread of six loosely twisted strands which can be separated and used singly or in any combination.

Coton Perlé or pearl cotton is a twisted thread with a rich, shiny appearance. It cannot be divided, but is available in three slightly different thicknesses: no. 8, the finest; no. 5, slightly thicker and most commonly available; and no. 3, the thickest.

Coats *Nordin yarn* is a new cotton yarn which is a very fine matt thread in a good range of colours and subtle shades. It is very similar to the Danish type threads so popular for fine crewel work.

Soft embroidery cotton is the thickest of the cotton threads, similar to some types of crochet cotton, with a dull, matt finish. It is a very soft thread and cannot be divided.

Tapisserie or tapestry wool is a non-divisible four-ply woollen yarn which is ideal for canvaswork and is available in a vast range of colours.

If the thread mentioned is not easily available you can substitute with threads from other manufacturers' ranges.

Embroidery Frames

Using a frame will be very helpful to you, and your embroidery will be more successful and have a professional look when finished if you do. It is not only easier to handle fabric that is held taut within a frame, but you will find your stitches are well-formed. If it is necessary for stitches to be of an even size or spacing, this can be done much more easily by using a frame. Also distortion of the fabric caused by pulling yarn or thread too tightly through the fabric is reduced to an acceptable minimum.

There are a variety of frames available, and the choice depends upon the type of fabric, size of project and personal preference.

If you do not have the exact size of frame available, but have something similar you will probably be able to make use of it. However, if you need to reposition the fabric on the frame while you are working, you must be particularly careful to keep the fabric clean along the edges of the frame as these quickly become marked through handling. A piece of spare fabric pinned over the frame with a cut-out window over the working area will help prevent the fabric from becoming soiled.

Embroidery hoops are used for small pieces of embroidery worked on plain-weave fabrics that will not become permanently distorted when pulled taut within the round frame. (Fabrics such as nonwoven felt or needlepoint

A circular embroidery hoop is ideal for small pieces of stitchery, repeat patterns and borders.

canvas are unsuitable, although even these can be used in experimental embroidery in a hoop.)

Wooden hoops are preferable to the less rigid plastic ones, and many different sizes are available. It is advisable to collect several sizes, as they are inexpensive and you can then simply select the most suitable one to use for each project.

Fabric tape wound around the outer ring of the hoop will protect soft fabrics and stitchery from the hard wooden edge. The extra layer of tape will also ensure that you get a taut working area, as it prevents the fabric from sagging while it is being worked.

Similarly, an extra layer of spare fabric placed on top of the working fabric, mounted in the hoop and then carefully cut away to reveal the area of stitchery, will protect the stitched fabric from the risk of being soiled during handling.

You must be careful when using a circular hoop with evenweave fabric to ensure that the grain of the fabric is straight so that your Cross Stitches do not become distorted in shape.

Rectangular frames are very useful for larger pieces of embroidery and canvas needlepoint. They can be made quickly and simply from lengths of whitewood 2×2 cm (¾×¾ in). The corners can be butted or mitred and held together with wood adhesive glue and nails.

Old, clean picture frames of soft wood can also be useful and inexpensive. Alternatively, use ready-made artists' stretchers.

I find rectangular frames most useful and have a collection of different sizes. You will soon find which you like best and gather a variety of shapes and sizes. When using a rectangular frame the fabric is stretched and fastened on this type of frame with staples or drawing pins (thumb tacks). Start at the centre of opposite sides and work towards the corners, carefully pulling and fixing the fabric so that it is evenly taut and secure on the frame.

Specialist frames (slate or rotating frames) are more expensive, but they can be of great use as they are adjustable and you can stretch fabric very evenly on them. They are useful when working a long thin strip of embroidery, such as a border for a towel.

REMOVING FABRIC FROM A FRAME

Once you have completed working your embroidery you will need to remove it from the frame.

If you have used staples to hold the fabric firmly on the frame then you will find it easier to remove them by levering them with a screwdriver, passing it between the staple and the fabric and frame. Then remove the raised staple with a pair of pliers. Take care not to push the sharp end of the screwdriver into the fabric possibly damaging it.

Do not be tempted to try to remove the staples with a pair of scissors, it is more difficult and you risk ruining your scissors.

If you use drawing pins (thumb tacks) to secure the fabric to the frame then lever them up with a screwdriver in a similar way.

ENLARGING A DESIGN

You will find that some of the designs in this book need to be enlarged to the correct size of working. This can be done successfully by the following 'grid' method, but accurate measuring is important.

Place the small design within a box and draw a grid of squares over it. Draw a larger box with the same proportions but of the required size. Draw the same number of bigger squares within this (see page 134).

Copy the small design, square by square, onto the larger grid, marking where design lines cross grid lines. Join up all these marks (see page 134).

A quick way of enlarging a design can be achieved by using a photocopy machine, many of which now have the capacity to change the size of documents and drawings.

I find a photocopier extremely useful as it can greatly speed up the design process, enlarging, reducing and repeating images that would otherwise take hours to do.

TRANSFERRING DESIGNS

Once you have drawn your design to the correct size or repeated it for a border pattern, you will need to transfer it from the tracing paper to the fabric. There are several ways of doing this, and it is important to choose the most suitable method for each project. For example, if you have a very fine fabric such as cotton lawn, there is no need to baste the design on to the fabric through tracing paper, as you will be able to draw it straight onto the semi-transparent fabric.

Always use the method of transfer that is suggested to you in the projects, unless of course you have chosen to adapt the project in some way.

The following methods of transfer have been used:

DIRECT TRACING ON TO FABRIC

This is a quick and accurate method, but the fabric must be thin enough for you to see the drawn design underneath it.

Draw a grid of squares over the small design, then draw a diagonal line through the grid, extending it to make a larger box of the same proportions as the small one, but enlarged to the required size.

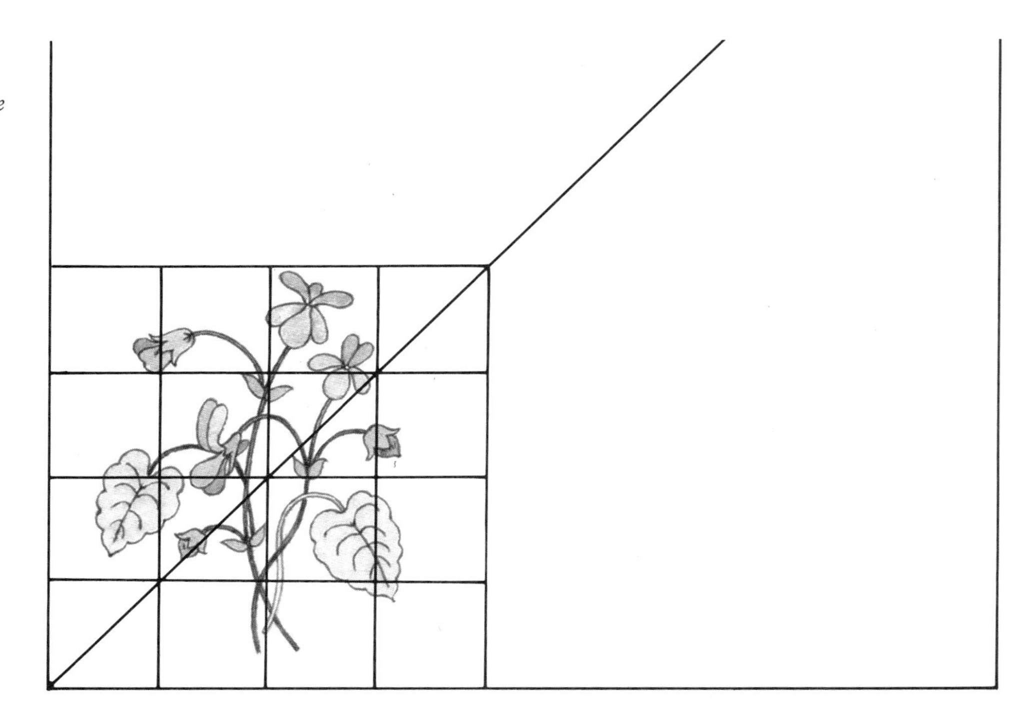

Then draw a grid of the same number of squares in the big box. Copy where the design lines intersect the grid lines and then carefully and accurately join them up to give the enlarged design.

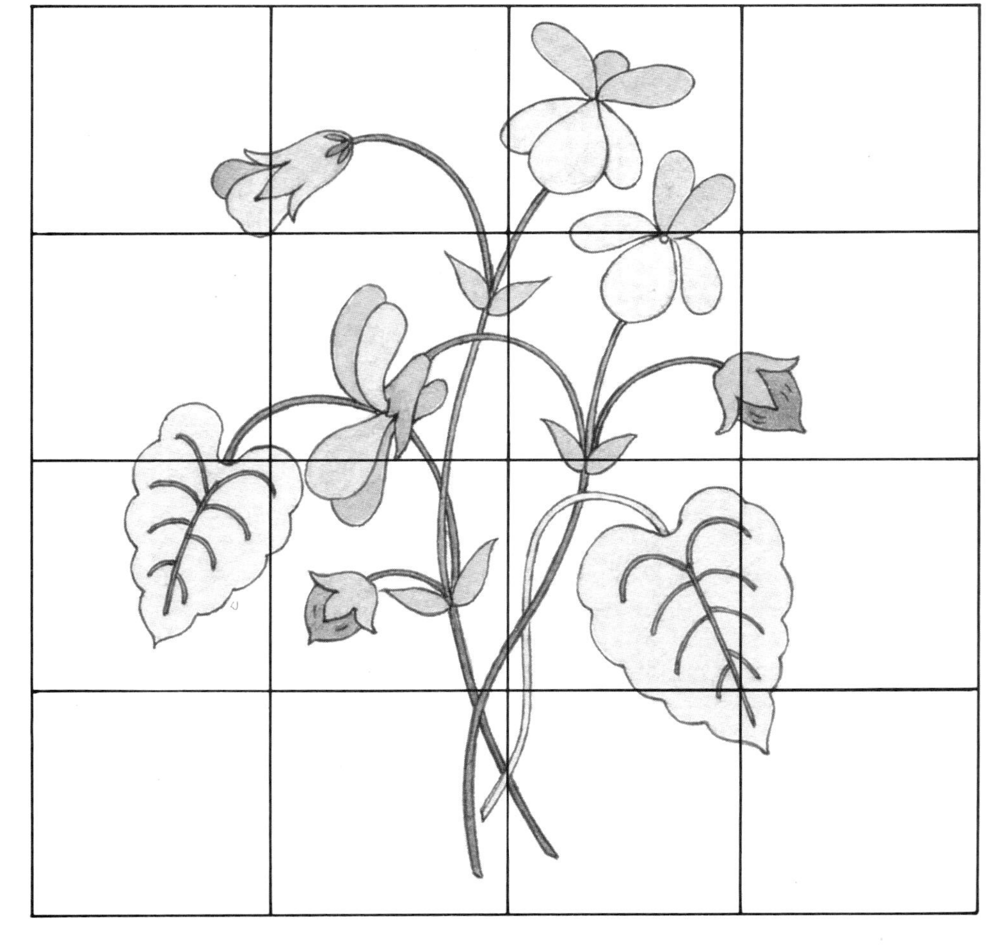

Always use masking tape to secure the drawn design on to a clean, white surface. (If you place it on a dark surface you will not see the design lines easily.) Then tape the fabric in position over the design so that it is smooth and flat. Then, using crayons or pencils of appropriate colours, trace the design lines carefully on the fabric. Remember to keep the crayons well-sharpened and make the finest lines possible on your fabric.

Never use lead pencil, ballpoint, felt-tipped or ink pens, as they all will leave blotchy marks on your fabric and will run if washed. The light use of crayons will not spoil the fabric, and they will wash out easily if the embroidery is laundered.

If you find it hard to see the design through the fabric, but wish to use this method, try taping the drawn design and then the fabric to a window. Remember, though, do not press too hard on the glass.

The canvaswork projects in this book are all worked from charts but sometimes they can be worked by drawing the design directly on to the canvas by the same method. However, you should use a waterproof or indelible marking pen to draw on the canvas, as you need a more definite mark than a crayon can give, and you will stitch over the marks. Always try to align straight lines in the design with the threads of the canvas, unless they lie at an obvious angle to them.

USING FABRIC TRANSFER PENCILS

These are useful if the fabric you are going to use is too thick or dark to see through. However, they must be used very carefully as their colours are quite strong, and it is sometimes difficult to use them for very detailed shapes. Always choose a pencil near in colour to either your fabric or threads to reduce the risk of showing under the stitchery. Always work with a sharp-pointed pencil.

The method is simple to carry out, but always make a test sample first to ensure it will be suitable for your particular fabric.

Draw the design in pencil or felt-tipped pen on tracing paper. Then on the underside, draw along the lines once more, this time with the fabric transfer pencil. Check there are no specks of pencil left on the paper before placing it transfer side down over your fabric. Then, without moving the paper at all, carefully iron over the design area, so that the heat of the iron transfers the design on to the fabric.

You can always draw/trace the design straight on to tracing paper using the pencil, then turn the paper over and transfer the design on to your fabric but remember the design will be a mirror image to the original (see Butterflies and Flowers Mirror Frame, page 76).

USING FABRIC DYE CRAYONS

There are several types of fabric dye crayons available from good craft shops, usually sold in small packets of at least eight different colours.

They provide a quick, clean and dry method of printing colourful designs on to fabric. Some of these crayons should be used on natural fabrics only while others are recommended for use with synthetic or cotton mix fibres.

The type that I have used in some of the projects in this book are known as fabric transfer crayons. They are used like transfer pencils to draw on tracing paper; very detailed and subtle effects can be achieved.

Draw the design on tracing paper using the crayons, mixing their colours as necessary. Then place the coloured design, waxy side down, over the fabric, and without moving the two layers, iron over the coloured area to transfer it to the fabric.

Points to remember when using these crayons:

1 Draw the design in pencil on one side of the tracing paper; then colour in the other side of the paper.

2 Use a synthetic or mixture fabric as fabric transfer crayons do not work well on natural fibres.
3 Always make a test strip of colour shade and strength.
4 Keep the crayons clean and with well-shaped points.
5 Do not allow smudging to occur when drawing with the crayons on the paper as this will show on the fabric.
6 Lightly brush off any specks of crayon left on the paper (any specks left on the paper will be transferred to the fabric and possibly spoil your work.)
7 Pin and hold the tracing paper firmly in position over the fabric. Do not allow the two to move against one another or a blurred effect will occur.
8 Always read and follow the manufacturer's instructions very carefully, as some types may differ from others.

TRACING AND BASTING

This method takes a little time, but sometimes it is necessary. For example, you may want to mark the shape or position of a design without marking the fabric with a pen or crayon if you were embroidering white fabric with white stitchery.

Draw the design on tracing paper using a fine felt-tipped pen. Do not use lead pencil or a ballpoint pen, as the colour may pass through on to the fabric when it is stitched and leave a permanent mark.

Lay the traced design over your fabric and pin it to hold. With basting thread, work small basting stitches through the paper and fabric along all the design lines. Remember your stitches will need to be quite small in order to show the design clearly on the fabric.

When you have completed the stitching, carefully score along the stitched lines with the point of your needle to break the paper. Then gently pull away all the pieces of paper, leaving the basting stitches on the fabric as a guide. Do not distort the basting stitches as you pull. Remember to remove the basting stitches if they show when your embroidery is completed.

USING A TEMPLATE

These are simple shapes usually made of thin cardboard or firm paper. They are made by tracing the pattern shape and transferring it to the cardboard. The shape is cut out and then used as a rigid pattern to draw around on fabric.

This method is particularly useful when the same shape is to be repeated several times in a design (see Pair of Patchwork Pillows, page 116).

WORKING FROM A CHART

With some canvaswork or evenweave embroidery, the most effective way of transferring the design from paper to fabric is by carefully following the design pattern, stitch by stitch, from a colour or symbol chart. You must work systematically when following a chart, and it is vital to keep checking that you are reading the chart correctly.

You may find it best to start in the centre for some designs, or at a corner, for example with a border. However, it is always advisable to find and mark the centre of your fabric with Basting Stitches and to have guidelines to help you transfer the design from the chart to the fabric.

Using a G-cramp

A carpenter's G-cramp, also known as a C-clamp, can greatly assist you if your embroidery is stretched on a rectangular frame. Without the cramp you have to hold the frame firmly in one hand, leaving only one hand free to stitch with. However, if you fix the frame securely to the edge of a table with the cramp, will you find that both hands are free so that you can stitch much more quickly and feel more comfortable.

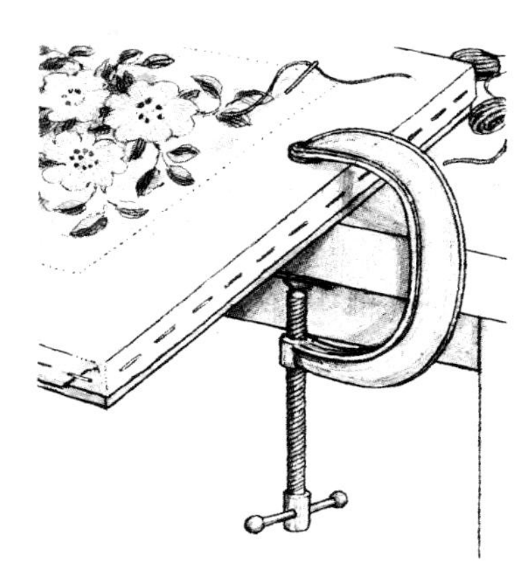

Using a G-cramp: with your frame protruding over the edge of a table and held firmly in place by the G-cramp, you will have both hands free for

Diagonal Basting Stitch

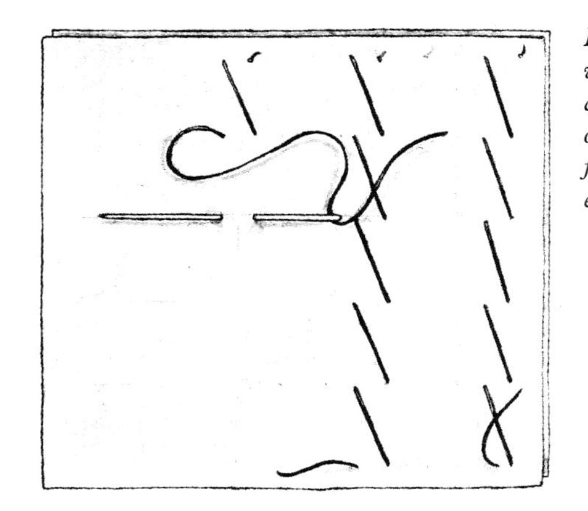

Diagonal Basting Stitch worked in several lines across two or more layers of fabric will stop them from moving against each other.

Basting is a technique that many people try to ignore. They use pins to hold layers of fabric together, thinking it will save time and serve the purpose of basting adequately. This may work sometimes but when you are embroidering through two layers of fabric held in the hand it is necessary to ensure the layers are held together and will not slip away from one another, causing puckering and possibly spoiling the work. This is a particular risk if using an embroidery hoop and you know you will have to reposition it.

Diagonal Basting is quick to work yet very worthwhile.

1 Smooth the layers of fabric together on a clean, flat surface, matching edges and wherever possible, the grains to prevent uneven stretching.

2 With a long length of basting thread, work lines of stitches (see above). Try not to lift up the fabric layers from the working surface, but stab the needle into the layers, lifting the fabric only a little, making a small stitch under the fabric and then moving downwards over the fabric to make a long 2.5 cm (1 in) slanting stitch.

3 Make several lines of basting stitches across the expanse of fabric at regular intervals approximately 7.5 cm (3 in) apart.

Cross Stitch

This ancient stitch is worked quickly and simply in two stages, with two diagonal stitches worked over each other to form the cross. Each stitch must be worked in the same way to give a smooth and regular effect, but it does not matter which way the upper stitch of the cross slopes, as long as they all slope in the same direction.

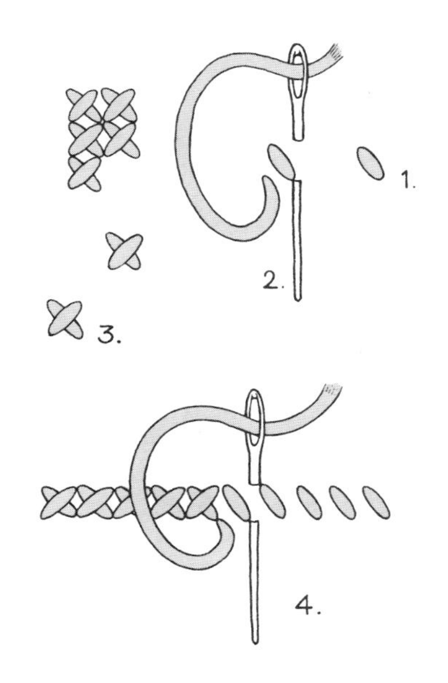

1 Half a cross stitch.
2 The second stitch of the cross being worked.
3 A group of completed cross stitches and isolated cross stitches. Note: all the upper parts of the cross stitches lie in the same direction.
4 A line of cross stitches worked by stitching the lower parts of all the crosses, then completing them by returning along the line, working the upper stitches.

It is a very simple stitch and easily mastered but do remember that if you are working your embroidery freely, without the use of a frame, there is a risk that you may pull the yarn too tightly when passing the needle through the fabric. This will cause a pinched stitch and uneven tension, which will spoil the overall effect.

The stitches can be worked from right to left, or left to right as you please. For the purpose of the designs in this book where there are often small and irregular areas of one colour, you may work in whichever direction you find easier.

Stitches can be worked as complete stitches (see steps 1 to 3 left), or they may be half-worked in one direction and then completed by working back in the opposite direction (see step 4 left). Remember that your aim is to achieve an even effect of identically formed crosses.

Making a Twisted Cord

Twisted cords in the same colour as one of the yarns used in a piece of embroidery will greatly enhance the work, as they will obviously match the colour scheme and yet are easy to make.

Cut three or more lengths of the chosen yarn, 2½ to 3 times the finished length of the cord required. It is always better to allow extra otherwise you may find your cord is just too short for its intended use! Knot all the lengths together at one end and loop them around a closed door handle (or get a friend to hold them tightly). Knot the other ends together securely and pass a pencil through the loop that has been made. Wind the pencil round and round so that the yarn twists. Continue doing this, keeping the yarn taut until it coils around itself when it is slackened slightly. Then carefully bring the two knotted ends together so that both halves of the yarn twist tightly around one another. Gently pull and ease the cord until it is evenly twisted. Knot the ends together to prevent them from unravelling.

A thin cord, suitable for edging a cushion or tie-back, can be made by using three lengths of Coton Perlé no. 5. For a thicker cord, use more lengths of thread, or select a thicker yarn.

To make a two-colour twisted cord use two groups of different coloured thread of the required length and colour. Tie all the threads together close to one end to join them. Then separate the colours so that the knot lies in the centre with one colour on one side of it and the second colour on the other side, and doubling the length of the threads to be twisted. Then knot the loose ends of each colour and make the cord in the usual way.

MAKING A TASSEL

Take a length of thread or yarn 91 cm (36 in) long. Fold this in half four times to give a bundle of threads (see step 1 below).

Take a second length of thread, double it and pass it through a large-eyed needle (see step 2 below).

Hold the double thread around the bundle of threads and pass the needle through the loop (see step 3 below).

Pull it up tightly, then pass the needle down through the bundle and cut it off at the end of the other threads (see step 4 below).

Thread the needle again as before, and take it around the head of the tassel, pass it through the loop, pull it up tightly and secure it by pushing the needle up through the head and out at the top of the tassel (see step 5).

Do not cut off these threads as they can be used to sew the tassel in place (see step 6 below). For a thicker tassel, use more threads.

Tassels made of yarn matching that used in a design will enhance the end product.

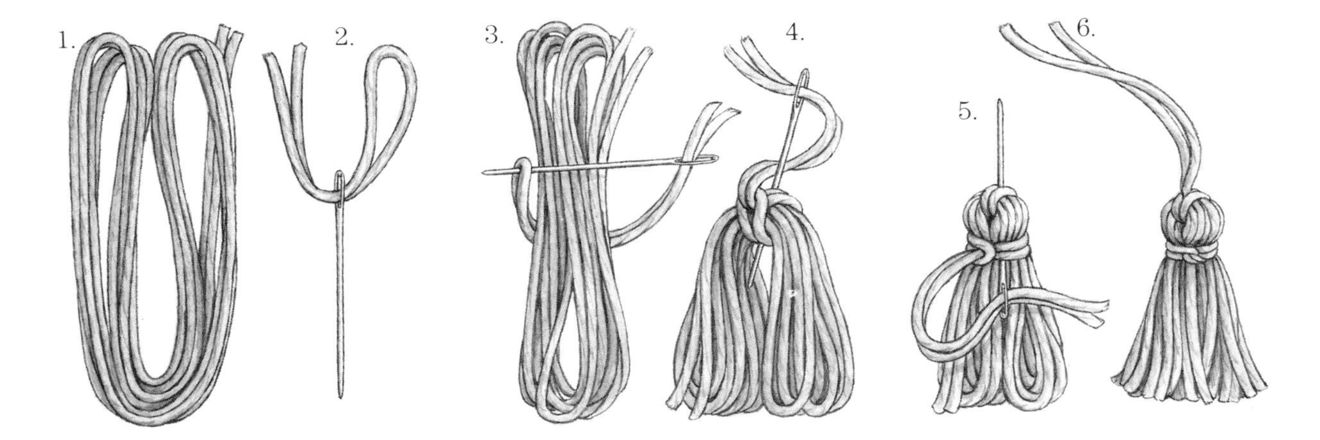

MAKING A GIFT CARD OR GREETINGS CARD

Use thin card that is firm enough to hold fabric within it while standing upright, but also thin enough to be folded easily. Choose the finished size of your gift card, remembering that you must allow a sufficiently wider border of card around the cut-out window to support the fabric.

You will need a piece of thin card large enough to fit the required shape (square or rectangle) within it, plus another of the same dimensions on either side of it. Lightly score the card dividing it into the three sections and fold along the score lines. Open out the card and accurately measure and mark the cut-out window shape within the centre section. Cut this out using a sharp craft knife. Make sure the window is centrally positioned widthwise, although it may be slightly nearer the top of the card than the bottom edge to give a pleasing effect.

The left-hand section becomes the back of the card and the right-hand section folds over the back of the card front to neaten it and hide the wrong side of the fabric.

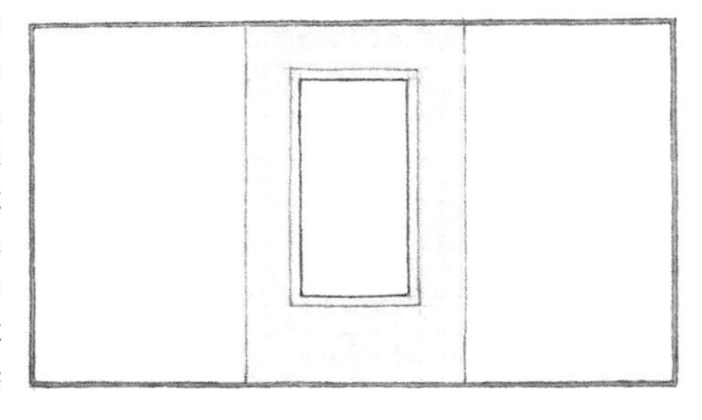

Divide the piece of cardboard into three equal sections. The middle section will have the window cut out from it.

Finishing Tips

All the projects in the book include instructions for finishing your embroidery. Generally, you should always remember to handle your stitchery with care, so that the fabric looks fresh and requires the minimum of pressing (if any).

If you do have to press your embroidery, *never* do so on the right side, as it will flatten and spoil the texture and finish of your stitchery. Always press on the wrong side, preferably with a steam iron.

Light use of spray starch can be effective.

If you need to lace your embroidery over a board to make a picture, remember to allow plenty of fabric around each edge of the design area for it to be folded over to the wrong side. Use cardboard that will not bend easily and strong button thread that will not break when pulled tightly. Also see right.

DAMP-STRETCHING

All of the projects given are worked with the use of a frame or hoop, so the need to damp-stretch finished work should not arise. However, occasionally you will find that fabric or canvas may become distorted during embroidery, and damp-stretching will be necessary to get it back into shape.

Everything must be colourfast and shrink-resistant and you should only use the minimum of water.

Place several layers of white blotting paper on an old board and dampen them. Then place the embroidery (right side upwards) on top. The moisture from the paper dampens the fabric, making it supple and thus allowing you to stretch it more easily. Use rust-free drawing pins (thumb tacks) to hold the embroidery in position. Gently pull and stretch the fabric back into its correct shape, working with opposite sides from the centres to the corners. You may find that you have to adjust the pins in order to achieve the correct shape.

Leave the stretched fabric on the board to dry in a warm atmosphere. Then release the fabric and you will see that the distorted shape has been rectified.

Remember that you must have plenty of excess fabric around the embroidered area into which the drawing pins (tacks) are placed, as they will probably leave small holes which can spoil the fabric.

STRETCHING AND MOUNTING FABRIC ON CARDBOARD

Always use rigid cardboard, otherwise you will find that it bends when the fabric is pulled tightly around it. It is preferable to use white cardboard on most occasions and try to use a good quality, acid-free board if possible.

1 Remove the fabric carefully from the frame without creasing it (see also page 133).

2 Cut the cardboard to the required size (if the embroidery is to be placed behind a window mount then you must allow for an overlap).

3 Trim away any surplus fabric around the area to be stretched, allowing at least 3 cm (1¼ in) on each side to be turned over to the wrong side or back of the cardboard.

4 Place the embroidered fabric face down on a clean, flat surface, then place the cardboard on top of it, centring it accurately.

5 Carefully lift up the cardboard and the fabric together and adjust their positions if necessary before replacing them on the flat surface. You will find it easier if you work partially over the edge of the table. Then with large-headed dressmaker's pins (glass-headed are ideal) and working along opposite sides simultaneously, gently pull the fabric to stretch it and pin it to hold by inserting the pins actually into the narrow edge of the cardboard. You

do not need to push the pins in very far, just enough to hold the fabric firmly in place.

When you have pinned the two opposite sides check that the embroidery is stretched correctly before proceeding with the remaining two sides.

6 Use a long, double length of strong buttonhole thread to lace the opposite edges of the fabric together. Work from the centres towards the corners, pulling the thread tightly and evenly (see right). Make sure you fasten off your thread very securely and only do so if you are satisfied that you have stretched the fabric evenly. Once you have done this you can carefully remove the pins from the opposite side edges.

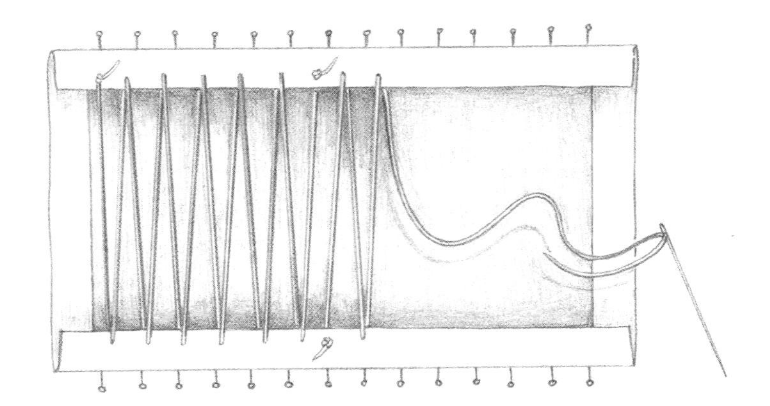

Then lace the other two edges together in a similar way. When you reach the corners, trim away some of the excess fabric and tuck in the remainder to create a neatly folded turning. Pull the lacing tautly, fasten it securely and then remove the pins.

Care of Embroidery

If you have used good-quality fabric and threads, your embroidery will last for years and years.

However, there are certain ways of prolonging the life of stitchery. Never place any embroidery in direct sunlight or near strong artificial lights, as both heat and light cause colours to fade and the fibres of fabrics and threads to weaken. Similarly, do not place embroidery near a heat source, as this will also make the stitchery very brittle. Remember, too, that a damp atmosphere can be equally damaging.

Frequent laundering should be avoided if at all possible and always use a mild cleaning agent. Gently reshape the article while damp and do not allow it to dry out completely before pressing it on the wrong side with a steam iron.

If you need to clean a cushion or some other article that may not be totally colourfast, then dry cleaning is essential. You will find that if you treat your embroidered articles with loving care and respect, they will require little more than a gentle brush and shake, or the use of the curtain attachment of the vacuum cleaner held over them, to remove dust.

Care for your embroidery as though it is an heirloom in the making. Enjoy it, respect it, but equally do not hide it away. Folding it and sealing it in a plastic bag will cause permanent creases which will in time weaken and break. Also, the lack of air will prevent the fibres from breathing.

If you must store your work for a long period of time, it is better if it can be stored flat or rolled smoothly (right side out), in layers of protective, acid-free tissue paper. Then it should be place in a clean fabric cover such as a pillowcase, and finally placed somewhere dark, dry and, of course, moth-free.

Stockists and Suppliers

UNITED STATES
Susan Bates
212 Middlesex Avenue
Chester, Connecticut 06412
(distributor of Anchor embroidery threads)

Binney and Smith Inc.
Consumer Affairs Department
P.O. Box 431
Easton, Pennsylvania 18044
(Crayola fabric transfer crayons)

DMC Corporation
107 Trumbull Street
Elizabeth, New Jersey 07206
(DMC threads, information and lists of stockists)

BITAIN
Binny and Smith (Europe) Ltd
Ampthill Road
Bedford MK42 9RS
(Crayola fabric transfer crayons)

Bedford Wool Shop Ltd
The Old Arcade
Bedford MK40 1NS
0234 355385
(full range of Anchor embroidery threads, information)

Dunlicraft Ltd
Pullman Road
Wigston
Leicester LE8 2DY
(DMC threads, counted thread fabrics, information)

John Lewis
Oxford Street
London W1A 1EX
(cotton fabrics, towelling, bed linen, embroidery threads and equipment, ribbons, trimmings, sewing threads and general haberdashery)

Liberty
210–220 Regent Street
London W1R 6AH
(plain and patterned cotton fabrics)

C.M. Offray and Son Ltd
Fir Tree Place
Church Road
Ashford
Middlesex TW15 2PH
(ribbons)

H.W. Peel and Co. Ltd
Norwester House
Fairway Drive
Greenford
Middlesex UB6 8PW
(Chartwell metric pattern guide paper – squared and graph)

The White House Picture Frame Studio & Gallery
47 London Road
Westerham
Kent
(picture frames)

INDEX

Page references in *italic* denote
illustrations or captions.

ACKNOWLEDGEMENTS

I would like to thank everyone who has helped in the making of this book. In particular I would like to mention Sue Storey and Patrick McLeavey for their book design; Coral Mula and Elsa Willson for their delightful pencil and crayon drawings; Paul Burcher of The Write Image for the jacket design; and Debby Robinson for the charts. I am especially grateful to Shona Wood for her superb photography which shows with stunning simplicity the stitch detail of every design.

Thanks also to Jane Judd, my agent; to Hilary Arnold, Barbara Bagnall and everyone at Ebury. A special thanks goes to Valerie Buckingham who always offered encouragement and support and who thoughtfully rearranged schedules to fit in with the birth of my son, Thomas. Finally, thanks go to my family for all their help and patient understanding.